D1011551

IF THE BOSS CALLS, I'M IN A
SAILS MEETING

IF THE BOSS CALLS, I'M IN A
SAILS MEETING

CONFESSIONS OF A BOATAHOLIC

JUDITH ARCHER

Illustrated by KATE SALLEY PALMER

Peachtree Publishers, Ltd.

Published by
PEACHTREE PUBLISHERS, LTD.
494 Armour Circle, N.E.
Atlanta, Georgia 30324

Copyright©1986 Judith Archer

Manufactured in the United States of America

Library of Congress Catalog Number 86-60007

ISBN 0-931948-90-8

Dedicated to my parents,
Fred and Mary Archer, who,
despite all the evidence to the contrary,
always believed that I'd do something right someday,
and to the memory of my friend,
Linky Leland.

Contents

IF THE BOSS CALLS, I'M IN A
SAILS MEETING

The Confessions of a Boataholic

The plight of the "boataholic" is something that folks in the boating business don't like to talk about, and as a result, many people aren't familiar with the term. While an alcoholic is someone who can't stop with just one drink, his nautical counterpart is someone who can't stop with just one boat.

Boataholism elicits no public sympathy. When the average wage slave is told about it, he mumbles the same phrase he always uses when told that boatowners have problems: "They can afford them." He pictures the boataholic as a loud, red-faced gent with crimson trousers, a funny little hat, a nubile blonde clinging to his side, and a magnum of 1959 Lafitte-Rothschild under his arm.

In fact, if your typical boataholic's face is red, it's probably because he's been upside-down in the engine room all day. If his trousers are crimson, it's because they're covered with bottom paint. If he's wearing a hat, it's probably pulled down over his eyes in the hopes that a legion of creditors won't recognize him. If there's a blonde clinging to his side, it's likely his wife trying to drag him home to do something about their house — which is on fire. And if there's a bottle under his arm, it's probably a domestic vintage — like a 1986 Schlitz. I should know; I'm a recovering boataholic myself.

My story is typical. Like most boataholics, I started out with social boating. Many of my best friends enjoyed boats, and joining them in a sail after work just seemed the friendly and sociable thing to do. No one ever told me that you could start out as a social boater and wind up a boataholic.

But such was my course. Before long, sailing on other people's boats wasn't enough, since they always wanted to quit long before I did. If a social drinker is someone who always uses a glass, a social sailor is one who always cranks up the engine when it becomes obvious that he can't get there any other way. Oh sure, they always had their lame excuses — gale warnings, icicles in the rigging, heat prostration — but I could see through them.

My childhood anticipated my boataholism. When I was only ten, my father rescued his oldest brother's 1917 Old Town canoe from the overhead of my grandfather's garage in western Pennsylvania. Stage one of her restoration took place on the Pennsylvania Turnpike, when the wind peeled all the old canvas off the canoe, which was strapped to the top of the family Buick.

After we got back to New Jersey, we called the Old Town people and soon UPS was delivering parcels of canvas, white lead, and paint. Over the winter, we re-covered the canoe and painted her a proper dark green. A couple of her frames had to be replaced; although the wood was still sound, someone had shot a hole in her bottom with a rifle. Back then, I couldn't imagine why anyone would want to shoot a boat. Now I know, for I'm certain that I spent more time working on that canoe than I ever spent paddling. And that's the way it's been with all my boats since.

I got more preparation for my malady as a young adult who took on several British sports cars, previously owned, one presumes, by British sports. Struggling with recalcitrant Triumphs (it was a considerable triumph just getting one started on a cold morning) and Austin-Healeys was a big step toward the obsessive tinkering that marks the boataholic. I had no idea that coping with the eccentricities of British cars was setting me up for the masochism of traditional boating. But I was a push-over.

I acquired a twenty-six-foot sloop. I began avoiding my former friends, whose enthusiasm for boating melted at the mere thought of twelve hours adrift under the blazing August sun. I began sailing by myself.

By this time, my sailing wasn't restricted to just weekends and holidays, and my work began to suffer. I started most days with a blinding headache brought on by using my skull as a boom-stop during unplanned jibes the previous afternoon. My hands shook from the nervous tension of trying to light a stubborn alcohol stove without scorching the entire galley. My eyes were bloodshot and bleary from salt spray and glare.

I began sneaking boating magazines to the office with me and disappearing into the ladies' room at frequent intervals to read a few pages to help me get through the day. "Weak kidneys," I would mutter in an attempt to excuse these trips. And although I'm ashamed to admit it now, there were times when I'd call in sick and go sailing instead. I thought that I had everyone fooled, but in retrospect, I've realized that sick calls placed through the marine operator were a giveaway.

Boataholism took me through one marriage and into another. I should have known that my first husband, who will have to be known in these stories as "Ecks," was not right for me when I saw his boat, *Whisper*. This twenty-six-foot Pearson Ariel featured just about everything that I loathed. And I always referred to it as my boat-in-law to make it perfectly clear that I certainly hadn't bought a fiberglass sloop with an aluminum mast, an ugly doghouse, and an outboard motor. I sailed about on *Whisper* wearing the biggest, darkest sunglasses I owned and a large straw hat that covered most of my face. Whenever I saw a wooden boat sailing my way, I went slinking below to hide. I was to find a better match in my present spouse, Eddie, a tugboat skipper, who

has helped me curb my obsession without destroying it.

But first my boataholism had to reach its full depth. I even got to a point where living aboard began to make sense. And I descended into a lower circle of the boataholic's dark netherworld, this one populated by yacht brokers and such who catered to the boataholic's weaknesses. By this time, I was hanging around marinas and yacht clubs, the only places where I could find kindred spirits who shared my bizarre belief that happiness could be found in a boat. Eventually, I would find myself living on a forty-four-foot house boat.

I grew increasingly alienated from my social sailor friends, who, whenever they bought a new boat, sold the old one. I was never able to do this, and within two years of my first sail, I was the proud, poverty-stricken owner of a thirty-eight-foot Matthews called *Serenity* and the twenty-four-foot schooner *Syren*, in addition to Ecks's boat *Whisper* — not to mention a fleet of ASV's (assorted smaller vessels) which included a kayak, a Blue Jay, a Sportyak, a sailing dinghy, and a couple of skiffs. I roamed the coast from Charleston to Miami restlessly and once came home with a Westsail 32.

Near the end of my boataholic days, I had a bout with the BT's, or boating tremens, which can take many forms, depending on what your boat is made of. I first experienced one of the most common varieties, in which I would snap awake in the middle of the night absolutely convinced that the vague rustlings and murmurings coming from beneath the hull had to be either teredo worms munching through the garboards, fiberglass delaminating, or electrolysis eating away at the underwater fittings.

By this time, I was spending the grocery money on boating gear that I would hide in the bottom of the laundry hamper. But I didn't reach my personal nadir until the morning I awoke to discover an eighteen-foot outboard with an eighty-five horsepower engine rafted alongside my little schooner. I knew that it hadn't been there the day before; try as I might, I couldn't remember buying it. I didn't even *like* outboards. If I had reached the point where I was buying boats during blackouts, it was time to get on the wagon.

I was told that one of the best ways to cure boataholism was to go public with the problem, telling others what had happened to me and what could happen to them. So even though I am not yet an ancient mariner, I tell you my tales.

Advice from
the Experts

When I first became interested in boating back in the late 1960s, I read everything I could find on the subject, little expecting to one day be writing about it myself. I read my way through the boating shelf at the local library. I subscribed to all the boating magazines. I looked for out-of-print nautical books at flea markets. I believed that if I read the experts thoroughly enough, I, too, would know exactly what type of boat to buy, when to reef, how to cook in a seaway, and how to perform the myriad tasks of a sailor.

I studied the gospel according to Street, Hiscock, and others and poured over the works of lesser gods as well. For me, as for many mere mortals, the words of these people were law. These writers had been places I hadn't been, done things I hadn't done, and their opinions had passed the scrutiny of supposedly knowledgeable editors. These were The Experts; all who sought the answers must turn to Them.

If I had any doubts, all I had to do was look at the photographs that illustrated their books and articles. Their boats were always immaculate. Their binoculars were always secured in oiled teak racks; their dividers, protractors, and parallel rules were lined up with geometric precision on the chart table, and a small arrangement of exotic shells, gathered during their circumnavigation, was usually displayed on the gimbaled table. My own boat, in comparison, usually looked as if a bomb had just exploded in the wheelhouse, scattering charts, books, tools, foul weather gear, and deck shoes. If Halley's Comet had scored a direct hit, the boat wouldn't have looked much worse.

It's hard now to recall exactly when my perception of boating authorities began to change, but I remember the first few jarring notes when a couple of cruising "experts" anchored their well-known ketch behind my boat in Key West. I was far too shy to approach these folks directly. After all, you wouldn't run up to the Pope and say, "Hey, John-Paul, I've read everything you've ever written and always wanted to ask you what your advice would be to someone who wanted to be Pope someday."

No, I waited until they had gone ashore in their dinghy and then rowed over in mine — a rigid glass one rather than the inflatable that these pros recommended — and took a closer look.

The first thing that puzzled me was the way they had anchored the boat. The nylon rode looked mighty small for the husky ketch, and the scope was unusually short. Still, when the wind swung into the northwest, as it frequently did in the winter, the ketch would not only swing into and block the narrow channel, but would also come uncomfortably close to hitting the stern of my boat, which was anchored on the other side. Since the anchorage was almost empty, I couldn't figure out why an expert would anchor this way.

The boat herself was even more of a revelation. In the photos I had seen, she was always spotless and gleaming with fresh paint and varnish. In real life, she was anything but. Her sails were sloppily furled, with only the most casual odds and ends of line holding them in place. Various lines snaked about the decks to no apparent purpose, and the end of each sported an Irish pennant. The entire boat was filthy with the grime of months of complete

neglect. The only explanation I could imagine, as I rowed in total disillusion back to my own boat, was that the ketch had been sold into bad hands. But no, I peeked through the binoculars as her owners returned and recognized them from their photos.

The seeds of suspicion sprouted and thrived. For the first time, I realized that my boat looked pretty spiffy in her pictures, too. By the time a forty-five footer has been reduced to a four-by-five glossy, any flaw smaller than a foot-square hole in the hull is likely to disappear. And even I could tidy up one cabin long enough for a picture; it was simply a matter of heaving all the junk into the next cabin. A photograph represents one frozen moment in time, not a way of life.

I began noticing other details. A photo in one of the boating magazines showed another well-known couple in the main saloon of their boat holding up their latest design for a macrame-covered widget of some sort. According to their writings, they had completely restored this boat. I'd read several of their articles outlining this restoration and had felt hopelessly inferior. I was trying to restore one of my boats, too, but my progress was discouragingly slow, whereas these experts had taken a bigger, older boat, in worse condition than mine, and turned it into a goldplater while I was still exorcising rot.

Or so they said. I looked again at the picture and did a double-take. Behind the widget, you could see a porthole that literally dripped rust. The ugly, wide stain ran down the side of the cabin. My spirits rose as my suspicions about boating authorities deepened.

Not too much later, another pair of cruising writers pulled into the marina where I was working. Their most recent article had described a system of hand signals that would allow them to approach a dock in dignity and silence while maintaining complete control of the situation. In the accompanying photos, the captain and mate looked calm and collected as signals were crisply given and immediately understood.

But the wind that day was gusty and shifty, and the clear,

concise signals shown in the magazine rapidly degenerated into a wild confusion of flapping hands and flailing arms that was finally punctuated by the first mate's screaming, "Are you going to slow this damn thing down or are you going to knock down the dock!" Actually, she used a highly descriptive term to describe the dock, but in all my years around marinas, I've never encountered a dock capable of performing the act she mentioned. Oh well, their theory was still sound enough.

Then I began seeing articles by a couple who espoused the alleged virtues of cruising in small, simple wooden boats. At that time, I owned *Syren*, a boat perfect for magazine articles. Constructed of Port Orford cedar on white oak frames, she was schooner-rigged and had no electrical system, no head, and no engine — all non-features that this couple strongly touted. *Syren* was, by any measure, a purist's dream, and I loved her dearly.

But she was not the ultimate cruising boat. Hardly. To begin with, *Syren* had what I call crouching headroom, just enough to tempt you to stand up, only to have a deck beam perform an impromptu prefrontal lobotomy. No electricity sounds fine until you turn the oil lamps up enough to read by them and discover that the cabin is hot enough to bake bread on the counters. And finding anything in a locker was like playing pick-up sticks in the dark. I always swore that the only reasonable headware on a boat like *Syren* was a miner's helmet.

Anyone who's spent the last decade trying to figure out the Federal regulations on heads has doubtlessly found the idea of reverting to the old cedar bucket appealing. The same couple claimed that this was, indeed, the answer.

Forget it. Can you really see yourself strolling casually below with your bucket under your arm in a crowded anchorage and then nonchalantly returning to the cockpit to dump your offering overboard? Or using the "facilities" when you have guests aboard? Or perhaps you'd prefer to imagine carting it up the companionway ladder in a heavy sea? No thanks, folks.

Well then, what about the question of size? *Syren* was a fairly

typical twenty-four footer, with an eight-foot beam and a three-foot draft. I'm 5′7″ tall, and Ecks was 6′ even — not exactly giants by today's standards. While we found little *Syren* perfectly acceptable for weekends and vacations, she could hardly be considered the ideal live-aboard for more than a munchkin. Several years later I learned that this smaller-is-better couple were both so short that they wore elevator deck shoes.

When they weren't fulminating against big boats, they were campaigning against engines. Now, I can argue against engines with the best of them. Engines are noisy, smelly, and expensive. Their shaft logs and stuffing boxes tend to leak. They take up a lot of room. Diesels cost too much, while gas engines can end all your worries about costs — or anything else — in the time it takes to strike a match.

Besides, with *Syren*, I learned all about wind patterns and directions. I learned about currents, counter-currents, and eddies. I learned to coax the most speed from whatever wind I could find. I learned to keep an anchor ready to let go at a moment's notice.

But I also learned to ignore interesting-looking side creeks — nothing worth looking at up there, I'd tell myself, and certainly no wind. I learned never to set out for a half-hour jaunt without first checking food, water, and stove fuel supplies. In fact, I learned never to set sail at all unless I didn't have to be anywhere for a fortnight or so. Most important, I learned that my next boat would have an engine.

I'm not the only person who started out proselytizing about life under sail, only to end up shipmates with a cast-iron jenny. But fortunately, I never committed these words to paper, which made them easier to eat when the time came.

I've watched as such mentors as Tom Colvin and the Hiscocks changed from a "who-needs-an-engine-anyway" stance to "maybe just a tiny one for motoring out of the doldrums" to a final "if we're going to have an engine anyway, it might as well be big enough to do us some good." In fact, those same folks who were such strong advocates of small, powerless boats are now building one that's twenty percent bigger — and rumor has it that they're trying to figure out where to hide an engine.

Obviously, at some point I decided that not only were these experts mere mortals like me but that I could join their ranks. I don't know everything about boating, but I've never let that get in the way of my forming some prejudices in most areas.

However, I'd probably still be doing more reading than writing if it weren't for an article that I read a few years back. The writer (I use the word loosely) and her husband had bought a new thirty-six-foot powerboat from a manufacturer in North Carolina and were taking it back to their home in the Northeast. This manufacturer formed flotillas of new boats and their owners and sent them off with a factory boat and crew leading the way. This crew did all the navigating and planning, made reservations at the marinas, corrected any mechanical problems that arose, and tied up first every night so they could talk the newcomers in. All the new owners had to do was follow in the factory boat's wake and obey instructions.

But you'd never know that from this woman's breathless account of their voyage. I've read reports of single-handed passages around Cape Horn that contained less hyperbole. At first, I thought that the piece was a satire on the adventure-cruise syndrome, but no, the author was deadly serious. She really surpassed herself near the end. First, she confided, "At no time was I actually in fear for my life." Remember, we're talking about the Intracoastal Waterway here, not the Bering Sea. And finally, after she was safe and secure at home, she actually quoted Whitman's "Oh, Captain, my Captain, our dreadful trip is done."

That did it. I dredged up my rusting typewriter from the depths of the hanging locker, freed up the keys with a shot of WD-40, and started writing.

Actually, the article wasn't a total loss. To this day, whether Eddie and I have been out for a fifteen-minute hop in the catboat or a fifteen-day trip in the tug, we rarely tie up without someone's intoning, "Oh Captain, my Captain," a doubtless improvement in literary quality over another favorite, "Home again, home again, jiggedy-jig."

So keep in mind, the next time you read about some flawlessly executed cruise, that boating writers, despite their claims, were not born with a tiller in one hand and a sextant in the other. All of us have been beginners, and those of us who write about our experiences haven't necessarily advanced beyond the rest of the crowd. We just tidy up our act a little when committing events to paper.

For example, I rarely — all right, never — mention the time Ecks and I pulled into a marina with me standing on the foredeck with bow and spring lines in hand, ready to jump to the dock and tie us up as usual. Just as we approached the dock, a man came running up yelling, "Throw me a line! Throw me a line!" Although I thought it rather inconsiderate of him — I obviously had my hands full already — he was so insistent that I picked up a spare coil of line and tossed it to him, then hopped onto the dock with my lines. It wasn't until after I had finished with the stern line and noticed the guy still standing there with the line in his hand and a bemused expression on his face that I realized he was the dockmaster.

It's regrettably easy, once you start giving other people advice, to forget that the same advice still applies to you. And so, as you read one of us "experts," remember that we aren't all that different from you. Most of us aren't sailing around the world on half-million dollar yachts. We've all gone aground somewhere along the line. We've all put off reefing until it's too late. We've bounced off of docks, and we've misread charts.

The only difference is that we give ourselves what every sailor sometimes needs — a second chance. When it comes time to write about our experiences, our keen seaman's eyes spot the shoal in time, the reef is tied in well in advance of the squall, and if we do clobber the dock, it's only because a friend was at the wheel.

This, we tell ourselves, is editing. Keep that in mind the next time you read an expert's account of pitching his mast overboard during a gale and saying to his first mate, "Excuse me, Sweetheart, I hate to interrupt you while you're preparing dinner, but we've had a bit of unpleasantness up here. When the hollandaise is done, could you please bring me our Yacht Emergency Procedures Handbook from Locker E-4, opened to page 67, "Dismasting at Sea?"

Before you start feeling too inadequate, remind yourself that this may not be *exactly* the way it happened. Truth may be stranger than fiction, but the way we "experts" recount our adventures is sometimes stranger yet.

Sleeps Eight Comfortably

Although I don't necessarily believe in the experts anymore, I still enjoy reading boating ads. It doesn't matter if it's a Burger in a glossy yachting magazine, a Pearson in the classifieds, or a Sunfish on a bulletin board; I read them all. Only recently, however, did I notice a certain discrepancy in these ads. While about ninety percent of the boats listed for sale are described with "perfect condition," "beautifully maintained," or "better than new," only ten percent of the boats in the average marina come anywhere near that description.

The light finally dawned one day as I was shuffling my way through the latest yachting publication while waiting for a root canal in the dentist's office. I was glancing at the ads but not really concentrating when one caught my eye.

"Shoal draft cruiser, fiberglass, simple sturdy rig, roomy cabin, excellent hardware and fittings. Perfect island hopper, reasonable." Sounds interesting, I thought casually, and then noticed for the first time the accompanying photo.

"My God," I yipped out loud. "It's the *Bic Banana*!"

It had been ten years since I had last seen the *Banana* hauled out at a south Florida boatyard. Although I'm usually pretty accurate at guessing a boat's age and background from her design, the only thing I could say for sure about the *BB* was that she probably dated back to the Roosevelt administration — Teddy's. I won't try to describe her lines: the name *Banana* did not invent itself, and it fit her (virulent yellow hue and all) like the proverbial skin. She was shoal draft, all right, since her centerboard had been removed years earlier, although whether by an act of God, man, or Mother Nature remains unknown. And her gaff rig could be called sturdy, after a fashion. Whoever had rigged her last had taken the expression "pole mast" quite literally, and her spar, along with most of her standing rigging, appeared to be courtesy of Ma Bell.

I suppose that she could technically be called a cutter, but there was a little something lacking in the design, and she never could be made to tack into the wind. Hornblower types might have enjoyed sailing her, since a change of course to windward required one to indulge in the now-neglected practice of wearing ship. Jolly fun, what?

By virtue of not having any bulkheads, berths, or cabinetwork left below, she was roomy enough inside. And I've got to admit that she did have some nice hardware, since one of her former owners was a notoriously light-fingered sort, and the boat was loaded with some of the most expensive blocks and winches known to man. None of it matched, none of it fitted, and none of it was quite in keeping with the character of the boat — although I'd be hard pressed to imagine just what that would have called for.

Fiberglass? Well, sure enough, at some point in her shady past, someone had slapped a couple of layers of glass over her decrepit wooden hull, but she had already washboarded badly enough that each separate plank could be counted, each butt showed, and there were gaps as wide as three-quarters of an inch (I measured once to win a bet) between the planks. Also, the outermost layer of glass was coarse woven roving, making the *Bic Banana* the

only boat I've ever seen with a non-skid hull. (I should probably point out here that the old *BB* did have some other, far more elegant name, but only her owner used it). And finally, as for the perfect island hopper, let's just say that I certainly wouldn't want to try sailing her to any island that wasn't within hopping, or at least swimming, distance.

So I came to realize that what the ad promises isn't necessarily what you get. Therefore, a few words of warning for those of you scouting the papers for your dreamship.

The first thing most ads mention is the boat's size. You might not think that there's much room for fudging here, but think again. Some owners — doubtlessly the same ones who give only their boat's waterline length when paying dockage — add on the boomkin, bowsprit, swim platform, and such when it's time to sell. My small schooner *Syren* measured a walloping thirty-six feet over all, and a couple of years after I sold her, I saw her advertised as a thirty-six footer.

But it's when you get away from the supposed absolutes that you really have to be careful. When the ad says "sleeps six," what it probably doesn't mention is that this is with two lying down in berths, two sitting up in the cockpit, one on the head, and one tied to the mast.

Beware of the ad that reads "a 30-footer with all the room of a 35-footer." This usually just means an ugly thirty-foot boat. Be doubly wary of the "30-footer with all the room of a 40-footer," which is a *very* ugly thirty-foot boat. And keep in mind that "cozy" is the common euphemism for no standing head room, while a "snug" cabin is one you have to sit down and slither into feet first.

Sellers trying to unload a slow, under-rigged dog sometimes fall back on the pleasantry of "easily-handled, comfortable cruiser." If you live in an area where the wind seldom drops below thirty knots and your spouse develops white knuckles whenever the boat heels more than five degrees, this may be just the boat for you. If, on the other hand, you prefer a fair turn of speed, the boat with the "excellent race record" may sound appealing — until you discover that it has eighteen sails, twelve winches, ten sail bins, eight pipe berths, and no head.

A boat's age is usually mentioned in an ad. When the subject is avoided, you can assume that the vessel in question has been around a while, and although you can ask its owner about its age, the answer is likely to be about as believable as Jack Benny's. "Classic" is just another way of saying "old," while "truly classic" is commonly reserved for antiques. Remember that "they just don't build them like this any more" may mean that they've finally learned better, or perhaps they've decided to start following their lawyer's advice. And when a boat is "one of a limited number ever built," perhaps it just means that this model didn't sell very well when it was new, either.

If you're in the market for something a little different from all the other UFOs (unidentifiable fiberglass objects) around the marina, an "original design" may catch your eye. How else would anyone describe a double A-frame rigged ferrocement trimaran? What about an "original cabin layout," a phrase I once saw describing a Colin Archer-type (which means a fat, slow, double-ender) that had its main cabin taken up by two easy chairs that featured seatbelts. "One of a kind," along with these other terms, should sometimes read "peculiar."

In this same vein, we have the "salty character boat," which evokes images of handsome, sturdy workboats of another era. Unfortunately, the "salty character" often turns out to be the boat's owner instead. I once wasted a couple hours searching for the "exquisite detail work" that an owner had promised before deciding that he must have meant the fairly well executed Turk's head on the king spoke of the wheel.

Unless you know how to interpret owners' remarks, you might as well ignore them. "Massively constructed" is often a cover-up for "crudely built," and "hand-crafted of beautiful Central American hardwoods" certainly sounds better than "built on the beach with a Bowie knife in Belize." "Built to Lloyd's standards" has a convincing ring until you discover that it refers to Lloyd Ferguson, East Bohunket's best brick-layer and house carpenter, who occasionally slaps a boat together when business is slow. "Will pass rigid survey" sounds promising, too, until you find out that this is true only if you hire the owner's uncle, Louis Rigid.

Maybe it's the phrase "just painted" that catches your eye. Aha, you think, no boatyard bills for a while with this baby. A used car analogy might be useful here. Think about it for a minute.

You've decided to unload your old clunker. It's got a lot of miles on it and the tires are shot. Also, the uneven wear is a pretty good indication that there's something out of whack in the front end. You decide that a new set of tires is in order. Do you tell the salesman, "I'm going to unload this lemon soon, so I want you to put the very best tires you've got on it"?

All right, then, do you really believe that the owner of this boat told the yard, "Be sure to do something permanent about those bleeding fastenings before you paint her. And don't skimp anywhere, I'm about to sell her, so I don't care how much it costs"?

Sometimes the problem is that you see only what you want to see in an ad. When a listing is shown "by appointment only," do you assume that this means they want a chance to screen out the peasant rabble, since no one with less than a triple-A Dun & Bradstreet rating could afford this beauty? It may be because the only time the whole boat is visible is at dead low water. When you read "elegant," you may envision a magnificent old Trumpy with raised and beaded panelling, teak decks, and bevelled mirrors, but the boat's owner may be referring to the velvet drapes his wife hung over the plastic ports and the imitation crystal chandelier in the stateroom. The same caveat applies to "unbelievably luxurious." This phrase was too true for one boat I looked at. I still find it hard to believe that anyone would lay shag carpeting over a wooden deck.

Since almost everyone advertises his boat as being "better than new," I always raise a mental red flag when an ad indicates that there might be some tiny room for improvement. If your boat "needs some work," will your first job be raising her off the bottom? Will the "handyman's delight" turn into the sadder-but-wiser man's nightmare when he discovers that the only thing keeping the planks together is the worms holding hands? When you read an ad that says "interior can be arranged to suit new owner," do you understand that this means that she's been gutted? And "needs some cosmetic repairs" may be true — most boats do look better when the cabin's attached to the deck.

Always beware of the boat that's "90% restored." Restoration figures should always be divided by a factor of at least five, and ten is often closer to the mark. Remember also that many restorers believe that when the boat has been torn to pieces, the restoration is half accomplished. Believe someone who's been there: boats come apart a lot faster than they go back together again.

Another common item in an ad is a bit of the vessel's track record. I read one ad where the owner touted his "bluewater" cruiser as having crossed the "Bay of Biscayne." You will note that this is a bit different, in several respects, from crossing the Bay of Biscay, but the water in southern Florida is indeed blue, and perhaps the owner thought that no one would notice the difference.

Sometimes would-be cruisers jump at the chance to buy a "proven circumnavigator." Before you grab your checkbook, however, consider this: would you be in such a hurry to buy a car that was advertised as "driven 150,000 successful miles"?

The bottom line is price. I'm always suspicious when it's not mentioned in the ad, figuring that the owner was too embarrassed to see his outrageous demand in cold print. "Unbelievable price" doesn't mean much, either. I'm a member of the post-war baby boom and can't claim to remember much about the "good old days," but I still find most boat prices unbelievable any more.

When the ad says "$35,000 firm," I figure that they're open to reasonable offers, while "$35,000 negotiable" drops the price another ten or fifteen percent, and "make reasonable offer" means that anything goes. However, be tactful when making embarrassingly low offers, and avoid statements like "You'd have to pay me to tow this thing away." All this does is antagonize the owner, especially if it's true.

On the other hand, I've acquired more than one boat way below its asking price simply by telling the owner that I'd like to buy his boat but just can't come up with more than a certain amount of money. (I usually have trouble coming up with even the amount I've mentioned, but that's another story.) Of course, it helps if you're dealing with a "motivated seller," one with his back against the wall.

Always remember that you've got to see it to believe it, which brings us back to the *Bic Banana*. I never would have believed that she was the boat described in the ad if I hadn't seen the photograph. So with all due apologies to everyone who's done his best to advertise his boat honestly and accurately, I offer a warning to boat buyers everywhere. When the ad reads, "Bl watr crsr, slps 8, clsc bty, ex cond, low $s," you may want to go take a look — but don't start buying charts for the Caribbean just yet.

The Name Game

All right, you've finally sorted through all the ads and bought your boat. Time for a new set of problems.

For openers, what are you going to name her?

What's in a name? According to the Bard, a rose by any other name would smell as sweet, but while this may be true for Romeo and Juliet, I'm not sure that it applies to boats. I've found that the pleasure of watching a handsome yacht plying the waters dissolves quickly when her stern comes into view and you discover that her owner has seen fit to name her *Sea Bitch*.

How do you go about finding a name for your boat? Many male owners quickly opt for the easiest solution and name the yacht after a member of their family, usually the wife. Although there's nothing wrong with this practice, which is common with commercial vessels, it does reveal a decided lack of imagination. Doctoring the name up so that it's *Lady Barbara*, *Miss Janet,* or *Princess Zelma B* doesn't really help matters much. These aren't bad names, but why not try for something more suitable and original?

Another variation on the name theme can be seen with boats

named *Sweet Sue, Lovely Laura,* or *Dotty Darling*. I hold Sloan Wilson personally responsible for a certain percentage of these names. In his otherwise marvelous book, *Away from It All,* he describes how his wife's perfectly valid objections to his purchasing an old wooden motor yacht dissolved instantly into simpering pleasure as soon as he told her that he would name the boat *Pretty Betty* after her. I don't really believe that any female over the age of twelve would actually fall for this ploy. And I may be a bit overly sensitive, but considering the excessive beam on some of today's production yachts, I wouldn't necessarily be flattered to have one named after me.

Some yachts can be named after a person better than others. As mentioned, fishing and other workboats are traditionally named after members of the owner's family, so if you own a former work boat like a modified skipjack, a Wittholz cruising tug, or one of Murray Peterson's lovely coasting schooners, you can feel justified in naming her after your wife, grandfather, or whoever. The serious nature of a working vessel is best complimented by the formal dignity of the person's full name, for example, the schooner *Susan B. Anthony,* not the *Suzy-Q.*

Another category uses the owner's name in original and presumably cute ways. Here we find *Roy's Toy, Dad's Pad,* and *Yessir, It's Esser.* Names of this ilk obviously vary from cleverly amusing to utterly dreadful, depending largely upon the eye, or rather the ear, of the viewer. *Roland on the River* is, after all, a pretty good pun, but what do you call it when Harold buys a Carri-Craft and insists on naming it *Harry's Carri?*

One of my peeves in the world of boat naming is the conglomerate. You've doubtlessly encountered many examples of the breed. When Ralph and Ruth and their son, Randy, decide to buy a boat, what inner demon compels them to name it *Ra-Ra-Ru?* When Ginger and Bob have enough good taste to select an extremely handsome trawler, why must they adorn her carved teak name board with an abomination like *GinBob?* Generally speaking, as the size of the family and the number of hyphens increases, the name degenerates proportionally.

Of course, you can always perpetuate one of boating's oldest jokes and invite your latest girlfriend down to see your yacht, adding shyly, "It's named after you." And when you get to the marina, of course, there's *After You* floating peacefully in her slip.

If you don't use a person's name for your boat, what do you use? The choices seem almost endless, but the best way to begin might be to consider the boat herself. What is her primary purpose? What is she like? Does her color, shape, or a particular design feature suggest a name? What do you hope to gain from owning the boat?

It should be apparent that while *Canyon Runner* is a good name for a fast, powerful offshore sportsfisherman, it doesn't make any sense on a fat, stubby, gunkholing catboat. The catboat would be better off with a name like *Simple Pleasures,* which would, in turn, be unsuitable for a seventy-seven-foot Huckins with all the amenities of a Park Avenue penthouse and enough electronics to embarrass the starship *Enterprise.*

Can you imagine an IOR racer named *Tranquility?* A three-story houseboat named *Flying Cloud?* How about a beamy, bowsprited, baggy-wrinkled ketch named *Shazam,* or a Bruce Farr design named *Old Timer?* Don't choose a name for your boat just because you like the sound of it; make sure that it also makes sense.

My elderly Matthews once went by the name of *Leisure.* I didn't particularly care for the name, which seemed likely to incite the rock-throwing peasant rabble into attacking the Wealthy Yacht Owner, but there were a number of tasks more urgent than painting a new name on the stern. One day as I lay in the cockpit in exhaustion and despair — I have never learned to face the discovery of new pockets of rot with equanimity — I heard a voice on the dock trill, "*Leisure!* What a perfect name!"

Thinking "What a perfect idiot," I immediately got out the sandpaper and paint and changed the name to *Serenity.* A minor change, perhaps, but accurate. While the old yacht didn't leave me much time for leisure, I had bought her with the knowledge that a certain amount of work would be needed and generally found living aboard to be a peaceful way of life. After all, rot, like the poor, will always be with us. In my own life, come to think of it, I've noticed a direct cause-and-effect relationship between the two.

Flora and fauna, both land and marine, provide a large pool of names from which to draw. You can choose a familiar one like *Dolphin, Sand Dollar,* or *Blue Heron* or make a more esoteric choice such as *Velella* or *Clione.* The name *Barracuda* would fit a long, lean, slightly sinister racer, but not a chunky motorsailer. On the other hand, I know a fellow who owned just such a motorsailer and also suffered notoriously poor judgment when it came to docking her. After considering both his yacht's portly shape and his standard crash landings, he decided to name her, with rueful accuracy, *Pelican.* Another chap with the same lack of boat-handling skills named his sloop *Harvey Dockbanger.*

Make certain that you know just what sort of creature you're naming your boat after. My friend whose last name is Hare was delighted to learn that there was such a thing as a sea hare. Envisioning, naturally, a quick, nimble ocean dweller, he decided to name his new boat *Sea Hare.*

Fortunately, while he was out sailing one day shortly before his new boat arrived, he encountered a strange bit of flotsam. It looked as if someone had combined lime and raspberry gelatin, poured it into a Frisbee to set and then, with good reason, cast the resulting mess adrift on the sea. Although the crew was unanimous in its opinion that this must be some variety of sea slug, a quick check in a marine biology textbook revealed it to be, as you've guessed, a sea hare. Sadder but wiser, my friend went back to studying his list of possible boat names.

Putting "sea" in front of almost any noun remains a popular method of coming up with a boat name. This may produce an ocean-dweller's name, as in *Sea Horse* or *Sea Cow* (which may be accurate, but wouldn't *Manatee* be kinder), or it may evoke a mood, as in *Sea Dream* or *Sea Fever*. Some people give their boats names which reflect other interests or hobbies. For example, there's *Sea Wedel* for the skier, *Sea Spelunker* for the cave enthusiast, *Sea Eagle* for the golfer, *Sea Scribe* for the writer, and *Sea Deuce* for the card-playing lady killer. Radio buffs might choose either *Sea Bee* or *Sea Q,* depending on their wave lengths. For the argumentative type, there's *Sea Here,* and for the exhibitionist, *Sea Me*. And finally, the owner of a ferrocement boat might opt for *Sea Mint*.

You can sometimes use your boat's material as a name source. One of the nicest examples of this I know of was the lovely old 1920s vintage motoryacht that well deserved her name of *Mahogany Lady*. I once saw a steel cutter named *Real Steal*, although I never knew whether this referred to her hull material or her selling price. Along the same lines is the teak ketch, *Stolsum Wood*. Using more modern materials, we have *Glass Slipper*, *Glass Lass*, and the ever-popular *Polly Ester*. Then there's the West system, which gave us *Foxy Poxy*. And finally, I've heard rumors that the builder of one ferrocement boat is threatening to name her, alas, *Ferro Fawcett*. I suppose it was inevitable.

Other people select names that refer to their yacht's country of origin, a practice that has produced some appealing names. Consider a Colin Archer design named *Svenska Flicka*, a Dufour named *Sortilege* or *French Leave*, a Dutch boier named *Zuider Zee* or *Dutch Treat*, the Argentinian *Gaucho*, or an Australian cruiser named *Waltzing Matilda*.

Sometimes it's the boat's shape that suggests her name. Thus we might see a Soling named *Sylph*, a double-ender named *Palindrome*, a fat, comfortable cruiser named *Tortuga*, or, in another instance, *Watermelon*, or the steam-powered cruising tug, *Well Stacked*.

Your yacht's color may be another source of inspiration. *Red Rover* for the circumnavigator, *Little Red Hen* for the single hander who has to do everything by himself, *Blue Moon* for the song-loving romantic, *Silver Lining* for the confirmed optimist, and so on.

But don't get carried away. I once had to find a name for a tiny black-hulled and white-waisted schooner, and, while admiring her swinging slowly at her mooring, I came to the conclusion that the only logical name, given her color scheme, was *Skunk*. Well, this was the boat that became *Syren* instead, but it took me a long time to stop thinking "Skunk" every time I saw her.

An owner may prefer to pay tribute to his boat's speed, or lack thereof, when he selects a name. At one extreme, we find *Greyhound*, *Flying Lady*, *Rabbit*, and *Fast Freight*, and, at the other, *Tortoise*, *Molasses*, *Patience*, and, a personal favorite, *Lethargy*.

Musical terms provide more names. If you own a heavy, beamy North Sea type whose virtues lean more towards seakindliness than nimbleness, you might want the name *Adagio*, the musical phrase meaning "in a stately and deliberate manner." *Allegro*, on the other hand, would make a fine name for a speedy, sprightly fin keeler.

The names of places sometimes become the names of yachts. Some places are real: *Minot's Light*, *Eleuthera*, *Statia*, *Tahiti*. Others exist only in imagination: *Rainbow's End*, *Oz*, *Shangri-La*, and, of course, *Fiddler's Green*, the sailor's heaven where the glasses are always full and the lasses always willing. Sometimes, the place is more a state of mind: *Faraway*, *Yonder*, *Over There*, and *Beyond*.

Names can have a regional flavor as well. From Downeast comes *Finest Kind*; from the Chesapeake, *Oyster Hoister*; from the Carolina Sea Islands, *Gullah Gal* and *JuJu Woman*; from the Florida Keys, *Conchy Joe*; from Louisiana, *Cajun Cat*; from the West Coast, *California Dreamin'* and *Pacific High*; and from the Northwest, *Rainbird*.

If you've built your own boat, you may want to select a name that commemorates that achievement. Some of these are rather obvious, such as *We Made It!* complete with dual meaning and exclamation mark. Another example is *My Way*, somewhat redundant on a catamaran fitted with what I can describe only as a double A-frame sharpie rig. (If you find that hard to visualize, please believe me that it's just as hard to accept when you see it in real life.)

Some are a bit more subtle but still obvious to those of us who have gone the do-it-yourself route. One of my favorites in this category is *Endurance*, whose owner confided that there were a number of times during the building when he wished that he had named her *Despair* instead.

I could sympathize, since while building my own boat I often thought about naming her *Never Again*. However, as an unsympathetic friend pointed out, she would, in all truth, have to be named *Never Again VII* or *VIII*.

Literature, fairy tales, and mythology are good sources. While *Nereia*, *Triton*, and *Aphrodite* are all appropriate yacht names, be careful to look up your choice in a classical dictionary before emblazoning it on the stern. A lot of boats sail around named *Valkyrie*, which is strange when you consider that the Valkyries were carriers of the dead. Do the owners of these boats know this, or did they just select the name because they liked its sound?

On the whole, however, more good names than bad are drawn from these sources. Think of a yacht with a long bowsprit named *Pinocchio*, *Cyrano*, or *Unicorn*, or a sprightly daysailer named *Ariel*, a portly motorsailer named *Falstaff*, or a Rosborough brigantine named *Horatio Hornblower*.

One day as I drearily contemplated the ramifications of my discovery of a long-term leak under *Serenity*'s rounded forward corner post, I hit upon the absolutely perfect name for almost any old wooden yacht: *Sisyphus*. For those who slept through classical literature, Sisyphus was the unfortunate soul who was condemned to spend eternity pushing a huge boulder up the side of a mountain. Each time he reached the top, the boulder would roll back down to the bottom and he would have to start all over again. If you've ever owned an old wood boat, no further explanations should be necessary.

The only thing that's stopped me from naming one of my boats *Sisyphus* is the certain knowledge of what name some of my cruder friends would use instead. If you've got friends like this — and everybody has at least one, and one is all it takes — use extra caution in picking a name. I know a man who bought a ketch named *Skua*, after a type of Arctic bird. He liked the name but gave up and changed it after several months of listening to his jovial friends call her "Screw-up" instead. I have a few much more colorful examples: none are likely to see print.

Regrettably, some folks have a penchant for offensive or scatalogical names. *H. M. Rhoid*, *Up Yours*, and *Wet Dream* are all in poor taste. I've noticed, not surprisingly, that these boats are invariably ill-kept and poorly handled as well, further testimony to their owners' boorishness. If you've come up with a name that you'd rather not have to explain to your ten-year-old niece, don't use it.

The name a man chooses for his yacht can be as revealing as any Rorschach test. Names like *Quest*, *Search*, *Battle Cry*, and *Sea King* would probably provide a shrink with plenty of insight into your character. Hard-driving Type-A personalities tend to favor names like *Challenge*, *Indomitable*, *Charger*, and *Decision*. Other, presumably insecure folks, have to let you know that they spent a lot of money on their toy and devise names like *My-Doe*, *Lotsa-Moola*, and that old classic, *Mama's Mink*. I hope that someday, somewhere, I'll meet a woman with a mink coat that she calls "Daddy's Boat."

Another variation on this theme involves giving it the reverse twist that implies that buying a yacht didn't have any effect on the owner's bank account. Names like *Small Change*, *Pin Money*, or *Lagniappe* are actually rather pretentious when attached to a million dollars' worth of Huckins.

Yachts' names sometimes involve what their owners do for a living. The lawyer owns *Miss Trial*, a doctor favors *Recovery Room*, the retired newspaper editor might like *Final Edition*, while an airplane pilot owns *Low and Slow*. My favorite in this group, however, is the minister who likes to fish and named his boat *Holy Mackerel*.

Sometimes a yacht's name provides a clue as to what her owner seeks to find with her: *Tranquility*, *Prestige*, *Adventure*, *Romance*, or *Solitude*. A word of caution, however, if you use a gentle, euphonious name like *Serenity*. You had better learn to slow *way* down when passing other yachts, and if you own a noisy generator you'd be well advised to learn to live without it in crowded, but quiet, anchorages. Otherwise, you're likely to hear your boat — and yourself — called an astonishing variety of names much more colorful but far less pleasant.

Sailors have always looked to the heavens, and many find names for their boats there. Stars, particularly the navigators' stars, have always provided names. *Aldebaran*, *Bellatrix*, *Capella* — you could almost run through the alphabet using them. Planets and constellations are also used, as are names like *Star Gazer*, *Star Sight*, *Starry Night*, and *Milky Way*. I suppose that *Star Wars* is another name we'd all better learn to live with.

When it comes to naming their boats, as in most other areas, multi-hull owners are a hard group to categorize. While many select names in the same manner as everyone else (you will notice that I've resisted the mono-hull owner's temptation to say "like normal people"), others prefer names that draw attention to the unique nature of their craft. And so, for the catamaran, we find names like *Mahi-Mahi* (one "mahi" per hull), *Twice As Nice* for the true believer, and *Double Trouble* for the disillusioned. On a tri, we might see *Tres Res*, *Triple Threat*, *Ménage A Trois* (I hope that this was reference to the three hulls, anyway), and the effervescent *Three Cheers*.

The origins of some names are rather obscure. The name *Pot Luck* on one sailboat puzzled me until I met the owner and discovered that he had practically stolen her at a U.S. Marshal's sale. It seemed that her former owner had been caught using her in the importation of Columbian agricultural products.

Then there's the elegant wooden motorsailer, *Onion*. I simply had to ask the owner how she ever acquired such a strange name. "The boatyard bills," he replied, "are enough to make anyone cry."

On the other hand, where did the lovely name *Silver Heels* come from? One of these days, I'll learn. Of course, the search for a euphonious name can go too far. H. L. Mencken once wrote that the most beautiful sounding words in the English language were "cellar door," and sure enough, there's a boat with that name.

Other names have a comic twist, as in the cheery *Sailbad the Sinner* or *Three Salted Nuts*, while still others have a vaguely Biblical tone, as seen on the converted whaleboat, *Fear Not, Jonah*.

Whatever you do, don't wait too long before naming your boat. Otherwise you may wind up owning a vessel named *The Boat*, or, if your wife's opinion prevails, *That Damn Boat*, or, if the youngsters have their way, you may wind up with *Grandpa's Tub*. He who hesitates to select a name runs certain risks.

Finally, let's not forget the dinghy. Most folks try to find a name for their boat's tender that is either a diminutive of the mother boat's name or one that will form a commonly accepted duo. In the first category we find *Tsunami* (or *Tidal Wave*) and *Ripple*, *Orca* and *Minnow*, *Big Dipper* and *Little Dipper*, and *Irish Rose* and *Rosebud*. In the second category, we have *Sunshine* and *Sparkle*, *Footloose* and *Fancy Free*, *Dark Cloud* and *Silver Lining*, and *Faith* and *Begorrah*. Some yacht and dinghy pairs fall outside of any clearly defined category. As examples, consider *Toy Boat* and *Toylette*, or the doctor's yacht *Pill Box* and her smaller companion, *Little Tender Behind*.

What if you've bought a used boat and don't like her name? Superstition to the contrary, I say change it. First of all, if you paid heed to all the superstitions surrounding boating, you'd never be able to sail at all. (What should I do, for instance, about the notion that it's bad luck to have a woman on board?) Also, you may notice that your wife, Gail, is getting a little tired of all the jokes about who *My Lovely Laura* might be. And, finally, you may feel that you've bought a boat whose name invites trouble.

When I bought my catboat, she was named *Carefree*, a fine name in many respects. However, some people can get away with names like that, and others can't. I am absolutely convinced that if I had kept the boat's name, Somebody Up There would look down on me and my little catboat and decide, "Hmm, Archer's getting a little too cocky again," before squashing me and *Carefree* like a couple of insignificant bugs. With all due respect, I changed her name to the more humble *Faith*, a simple, propitiary name that reflected her Puritan New England heritage.

Come to think of it, the only boat whose name I didn't immediately change was a small Scottish cutter with the unlikely name of *Ard Chuan*. That was her name when she was christened in 1930, and today, many owners after me, that is still her name. I think that the reason that no one changed it was simply that no one ever knew what language it was, let alone what it might mean. With *Ard Chuan*, superstition has always won out. Who knows what might happen if you offended some ancient Druid by changing her name to *Frisky II* or whatever?

But if the handsome cruiser you just bought is cringing under the name *E-Z-Duz-It*, I don't think that you have much to lose by changing it. After all, it's your boat.

In fact, that applies to all the suggestions here. While I personally believe that a boat should have her own name, if you've always wanted to name one after your wife, go ahead. (I should perhaps confess right now that my husband, Eddie, owns a tug named *Judith R*.) I think that you should select a name that fits the boat, but if you elect to name your Sunfish *Sovereign of the Seas* and can find room on the hull for all those letters, more power to you. I don't like the practice of deciding on one name and using it for all your subsequent boats, but if *Chug Chug* was the name you gave to your baking powder-powered submarine that you used to command in the bathtub, and you've used that name on all your boats since then, including your new fifty-eight-foot

Hatteras, so be it.

I remember an afternoon spent discussing boat names with Chuck and Eloise aboard their handsome Winthrop Warner-designed motorsailer. I was trying to decide what to name a vessel that was nearing completion and desperately needed a more dignified name than "The Hulk," which was what I'd gotten into the habit of calling her ever since taking delivery of her bare hull. Chuck raised his glass and began a dissertation on naming yachts.

"It's simple," he declared. "There are four main rules. The name should be short. It should be in English. Anyone should be able to pronounce it correctly. Everyone should understand what it means."

It made sense to me. I was nodding my agreement when suddenly I stopped short. The name of his boat was *Fale*. Although there's no accent over the "e," it's pronounced "folly." The language was Samoan, and it means, roughly, "home." I stared at Chuck accusingly.

"Well," he conceded with a shrug, "you've got to admit that one out of four ain't bad."

Malice De Mer

It's strange how you draw a mental picture of a boat and its crew from hearing its name. I was listening to the VHF one day when a boat named *Ocean Conqueror* called the local Coast Guard. *Ocean Conqueror!* Can't you just picture her with her crew of Captain Macho types, brawny and bare chested, squinting towards the horizon and clenching pipes in their teeth?

Well, maybe not. It turned out that the entire crew was so seasick that they wanted the Coast Guard to come and take them off the boat. Sounds to me like the ocean won that round.

I could sympathize with them, though. One of my earliest childhood memories is the annual family outing when over the river and through the woods to Grandmother's house we'd go. Over the years, we established some traditional stopping points: the country butcher's where they cured deliciously smoky Pennsylvania Dutch bacon, the Amish orchard that grew the world's best peaches, and the inevitable point, usually halfway across the Delaware River, at which I'd get carsick. It reached the point where my mother would start asking, "Do you feel all right?" as soon as we approached the river, and of course, once she got me thinking about it, I didn't.

This did not bode well for me when I first took up sailing. Fortunately, I started out in the relatively sheltered waters of Charleston Harbor. The harbor can kick up a nasty chop when the wind opposes the current, but I wasn't affected by this motion and came to the somewhat premature conclusion that I didn't get seasick.

Happy in my ignorance, I allowed myself to be inveigled into joining a dependents' cruise on an ocean-going minesweeper. I climbed aboard merrily with a group of wives, children, and Sea Scouts. None of us had ever considered what the lusty spring breeze might have in store for us.

The mob on deck did thin out rather dramatically as we pitched our way out the jetties, but I assumed that they were merely touring the ship. However, popular rumors of the captain's sadistic tendencies were soon confirmed when he opted to anchor the ship for the big cookout on the stern. It was slack water by then, and the ship promptly lay head to the wind and broadside to the long, greasy swells that rolled in relentlessly from the open Atlantic.

About this time, I sought out the head and, wandering through the wardroom, came upon a scene straight out of Purgatory. Groaning, moaning bodies lay scattered like fallen leaves. As I came within earshot of the head itself, I decided that I didn't really need to use the facilities after all.

I beat a rapid retreat to the open spaces of the deck and stood there gulping air like a goldfish out of water for a minute or two. Standing amidships and gazing over the side, I stared pensively at the horizon as it rose and fell. And rose and fell yet again before I noticed a sudden weakening in my knees, saw a vision of the Delaware River swimming before my eyes, and heard again that old familiar refrain.

"Do you feel all right?"

It wasn't my mother's voice this time, but rather that of a worried-looking officer.

"Certainly." I tried to sound convincing, for my own sake as much as his. "I'm just a little tired of standing."

"I'll get you a chair."

"Oh, that won't be necessary. I'll just make myself comfortable right here," I said, trying to look nonchalant as I slid down onto the deck.

Fortunately, the captain soon decided — thank God — to get underway again. I managed to heave (poor choice of words) myself back onto my wobbly legs and maintain the pretense that I'd simply been resting, thank you. But since I was the only guest on board who managed to avoid utter disgrace, I acquired a reputation for having a sound set of sea legs.

It's too bad that I persisted in believing this myself, since it led me directly into more trouble when a Canadian couple asked me if I'd like to crew for them on an offshore jaunt to Florida in their schooner.

My first mistake was in accepting their offer. My second was in assuming that since they had already brought their boat down from the Maritimes, they must have known what they were doing. The third mistake was theirs: they thought that *I* knew what I was doing.

With all our illusions firmly in place, we headed offshore, where, as the wind rose, I discovered that our illusions were the only secure items on board, and they were about to come adrift as well.

As the shore line disappeared, so did the first mate.

"Where's Jean?"

"Below in her berth. She always gets too sick offshore to do anything else."

Well, this was certainly a fine time to mention it. Before I could make an appropriate response, a mighty crash echoed from below.

"You might want to go below and see if everything's secure down there."

It would have been more accurate to ask if *anything* was secure. Lurching down the companionway, I felt as if I were

being shaken inside a giant rattle. The only things that weren't airborne, it seemed, were the bulkheads.

I stashed what I could, following the "break" theory of stowage: Would the item in question break if it got loose? And, more important, would it break me if I got in its way? I carefully tucked a few particularly fragile items under the first mate and tossed a few heavy things on the floor before I noticed that I was beginning to feel enveloped by an alarming feeling of stuffiness. I decided that the rest of the stowing had better wait.

I hadn't been back on deck for five minutes before the captain announced pointedly, "I sure could go for some breakfast."

I managed, with difficulty, to resist the temptation to tell him just where he could go for it and descended again into the maelstrom.

Peering into the depths of the big icebox, I discovered that the drain wasn't working and the box's contents were sloshing about in a foot or so of water. I grabbed for the eggs, only to have them go surfing out of reach. My timing improved on the second pass, and I bagged the bacon on the third. The butter would have to wait; hanging over the edge of the box with my head on a level with my knees wasn't doing anything good for my equilibrium.

The schooner was cursed with an alcohol stove, and the charred woodwork surrounding it didn't exactly inspire confidence. Surprisingly, it lit on the first try without starting a major conflagration, although this later proved to be beginner's luck.

Trying to ignore the cloying alcohol fumes, I soon had the bacon swimming sluggishly in a pool of grease in one pan and the butter melting for the eggs in the other. The swimming bacon was already beginning to set off sympathy waves in my stomach, and when I broke the eggs into their pan, they added to my distress by doing lop-sided figure eights.

Quickly realizing that it was time to look elsewhere, I considered the view out the galley portlight. One moment, there was nothing but heaving sea, and then we would rroollll . . . back the other way, leaving a view of tumbling clouds, and then we would rrrollll slowly back . . . to nothing but tossing sea.

Drenched in a foreboding cold sweat, I lept up the companion-way. As if out of the past came the words I'd learned to dread.

"Do you feel all right?"

"I just came up to tell you that breakfast's almost ready," I lied, while taking deep breaths and trying to find something to look at that wasn't moving.

I tumbled back below just in time to witness the mate, over-come by bacon fumes, bolt for the head. I gave her a nine for effort and a two for style: she almost made it.

Sad to say, this first morning set the tone for the remainder of the trip. On top of everything else, it soon became obvious that we were lost, and a cold front dropped the temperature below freezing. I thought that I knew what cold was, having spent my formative years trekking across the frozen tundra of northern New Jersey after my various sports cars stranded me in the boondocks. (Contrary to popular opinion, boondocks still exist in Jersey, although they're probably about filled up with broken-down British cars by now.)

The mate and I mutinied, and we put in at St. Mary's River, although the captain was under the impression that it was the St. Johns. My spirit of adventure had waned considerably in the past few days, and I took a Greyhound home.

Although I had learned several things on this outing, I had once again managed to avoid actually hanging over the rail calling on the great sea god, Roark, and therefore still clung to my belief that I was immune to seasickness. I figured that, as in horseshoes, "close" didn't count.

It was a year or two later that I moved aboard *Serenity*, that nice old boat with only one bad habit. She rolled. I could always pick her out in a line of boats at any distance; on the calmest of days, when other boats appeared to be moored in concrete, *Nity* would still be gently rolling. It didn't take much to set her off. One of the ship's cats crossing the pilothouse was enough for a half hour's continuous rocking. Eventually, I came to regard this incessant motion as sort of a nervous twitch, similar to the habit some folks have of constantly drumming their fingers or tapping their toes.

It wasn't until Ecks and I took a cruise to Dry Tortugas that *Serenity*'s nervous habit developed into a full-blown psychosis. We had a beam wind, which would have been lovely if we had been sailing. But we weren't sailing, and we also had a beam sea, which was anything but lovely. *Serenity* really put her shoulder into it and wallowed delightedly through the deep blue water.

We had barely cleared Key West when I was summoned from the galley by the announcement, "Your cat just threw up on my chart."

I found the semantics interesting. Suddenly the cat had become "my" cat, while the chart had become "his" chart. I cleaned up the results as best I could, and although the Kitty Krunchies had been but little altered by their brief stay inside the cat, my own stomach began doing somersaults.

I was distracted from my woes, however, when I asked, after a couple of truly spectacularly deep rolls, just what kept an unballasted powerboat from rolling right over.

"Nothing."

Well, that was certainly interesting to know. But if anyone ever tries to tell you that seasickness is all in your head, you may feel free to cite my cats. Both of them were wretchedly ill the entire day. One, after throwing up on the chart as a demonstration of what he thought about the whole exercise, retreated to the forepeak and suffered there in martyred silence. The other put on a show worthy of Camille. Hooking one claw in the pilothouse carpet as a pivot point, he allowed the rest of his body to roll listlessly back and forth with the waves. His eyes glazed over, his mouth gaped open, and his tongue lolled out on the carpet in a sad pink ribbon. It was a piteous sight.

For a variety of reasons, including the queasy cats, the powerboat experiment didn't last too long, and soon I was looking for another sailboat. I had about decided to build a Herreschoff

Nereia when I did a typical 180° turn and settled on a Westsail 32 instead.

Before making a final decision, Ecks and I wanted to visit the plant and take a test sail, so we drove non-stop for 900 miles in a VW bug to the Westsail factory. It was rather late when we arrived, and the only place still open for dinner was a rather seedy-looking seafood restaurant. In honor of our future cruising plans, we ordered the Offshore Platter.

The name was indicative of the results, all right. I spent the balance of the night hanging over the motel room's equivalent of a lee rail.

Morning found me feeling distinctly wan but eager to be off to the factory nonetheless. I had passed on breakfast, which was probably wise, and settled instead for several cups of black coffee, which was not. We spent some time tramping around the factory, which was heady with fiberglass fumes, and then headed for the marina.

"We'd better hurry," Karl, the salesman, said. "I want to get out the inlet before the tide turns against this wind."

I could understand his concern as we punched our way out the narrow, shoal-surrounded slot through already steep seas. But it was a glorious spring day, the boat was in her element, and I was enjoying myself thoroughly until we came about and headed back in.

"I want you to see how the steering vane handles these cross seas."

I had always been fascinated by steering vanes, until that day. The Westsail stopped pitching and started wallowing. As the horizon rose, swung, and fell, the vane itself flipped and flopped in another pattern, while my stomach rolled about in yet another rhythm. As the great, greasy swells loomed up alongside the cutter, they picked her up and passed on, leaving her to fall in a familiar roller coaster slide into the trough. I decided that it was time to look elsewhere, but unfortunately, the only alternative views were the bowsprit etching figure eights over the same lurching horizon or the mast arcing wildly across a turbulent sky.

"Do you feel all right?" This time the voice was Karl's, whose visions of a healthy commission were fading as fast as my color.

"Sure."

Of course, now that he had mentioned it, sure was precisely what I no longer was.

"You look sort of green. You don't get seasick, do you?"

Ecks, roused from reveries of distant waters, rushed to my defense.

"She *never* gets seasick."

He regarded me somewhat curiously.

"You know, you are turning sort of green, though. I always thought that was just a figure of speech."

"It's just a reflection off the water." I really didn't feel like discussing it.

Karl, who had been sitting directly across from me on the lee side of the cockpit, beat a discreet but hasty retreat to the fore-deck while I tried to calculate the distance to sheltered water.

I made it without disgracing myself, although there was admittedly little time to spare. Much to Karl's surprise, we did buy the boat, and I convinced myself that it must have been the offshore platter, not the offshore cutter, that had done me in.

Eventually, I even learned that there are times when a seasick passenger can be an asset. I'd accepted a job as cook on a tugboat, which I assumed stayed within the sheltered confines of the Intracoastal Waterway. The next thing I knew, we were headed offshore with a bargeload of tires in tow.

The plan called for us to dump half the load on an artificial fishing reef ten miles offshore, and the other half on another reef that was within spitting distance of the beach. On board with our regular crew were two representatives of the State Wildlife Department.

One of these men, Wyatt, was the veteran of a number of these expeditions; and although he enjoyed fishing from small boats, he had never learned to endure the exuberant motion of the tug in a seaway. Resigned to his fate, he had gotten into the habit of retreating to his berth immediately after boarding and remaining there until the tug crew came and carried him back to dry land. In the meantime, he didn't care where, when, or, I suspect, even *if* we dumped the tires.

But this time he was accompanied by his new boss, Charlie. We sized this fellow up quickly. Pale and portly, balding and bespectacled, he didn't look as if he'd give us much trouble once we started rolling. We should have known that looks can be deceiving.

By the time we reached the first reef, the wind was howling, the barometer was dropping, and the tug was taking a considerable beating. Before long, it became apparent that we wouldn't be able to finish both jobs before dark. None of us wanted to spend the night anchored offshore, but none of us was any too eager to run down on an unlit lee shore in the dark, either.

None of us except Charlie, that is. We tried to explain to him the advantages of dumping this entire load on the offshore reef and the next load on the inshore site, but he wasn't buying it. The captain decided that it was time for drastic measures and pulled me aside.

"What's for dinner?"

"I was planning on roast chicken."

"What else could you fix?"

"Fried pork chops?" My stomach lurched along with the tug at the very thought.

"Say, do you feel all right?"

"Sure."

The crew had pinned their hopes on my getting Charlie so sick that he would allow us all to go home, so I didn't bother trimming the fat off the suety chops before dropping them in a pan of seething bacon fat. I judiciously added an extra chunk of fatback to the vegetables, fried potatoes in stale oil, and finished up by making a gravy greasy enough to match the oil slick left by the *Torrey Canyon*. By the time this indigestible mess was ready, we had the tug tethered behind the anchored barge, where she was rolling her scuppers under with wild abandon.

"Chow's down," I croaked in a voice that was definitely more hollow than hearty. Charlie charged into the galley, sniffing the air hungrily, while the rest of our crew straggled in with a notable lack of enthusiasm.

"Oh boy! Pork chops! My favorite!"

Charlie piled his plate high, then drowned everything in a sea of greasy gravy. We all watched in disbelief and despair as he wolfed it all down and then went on to eat Wyatt's share as well.

"Just like Mom's cooking," Charlie burped happily. I made a note never to accept an invitation from Charlie's mom for a home-cooked meal. But we had met our match; we would spend the night at anchor.

Charlie slept like a babe in its mother's arms; the rest of us didn't fare so well. Having spent a little too long watching the fatty chops doing sluggish laps across the grease-filled skillet, I had wisely declined to sample my own cooking and was spared the struggle for position at the rail. When my suffering shipmates turned on me, I modified Kipling a bit and quoted, "If you can keep your dinner while those around you are losing theirs and blaming it on you . . ." They were even less impressed with my erudition than my cuisine. On the other hand, Eddie (my future husband) was the captain of that tug, and he decided that anyone who could cook at all under those conditions was worth keeping on a permanent basis.

It did seem as if I was winning my personal battle against *mal de mer* through the power of negative thinking. For one thing, having stated so emphatically that I did *not* get sick, I felt compelled to live up to my claim, particularly since I was always surrounded by people who would never, ever, let me forget it if I did succumb.

Another advantage was that since I convinced everyone that I didn't feel the least bit bothered in a seaway, they tended to take my word for it and leave me alone. Human nature can be ugly, and if your crewmates find out that you suffer from landlubber's legs, they will immediately divide into two groups.

First, we have those downright sadistic types who probably enjoyed pulling the wings off flies as youngsters and who, for all I know, may still enjoy doing so. The moment you begin to pale, they start making supposedly humorous remarks like, "Wouldn't a liverwurst on rye with gobs of mayo and raw onion taste good about now," or "Want to give that chum bucket a stir?"

Worse, perhaps, are those well-meaning souls who offer various home remedies for your malaise.

"Go below and lie down."

"Try biting into a lemon."

"The best thing to settle your stomach is a shot of straight gin."

Or, I suppose, you could do all three things at once, which would at least get you past that "I feel like I might throw up" stage in a hurry.

Now, those of you who do suffer from seasickness are undoubtedly aware of various medically approved remedies for your condition. I tried one such preparation early on in my boating life. It did, to be sure, prevent my feeling the first touch of nausea. On the other hand, since I spent the entire day sleeping in the scuppers, I felt that I had gained little in the experiment.

Recent progress has been reported on this front, largely as an offshoot of the space program. I've met a number of folks who swear by the dot-behind-the-ear, band-on-the-wrist cures for this ancient malady, which should come as good news to other sufferers who would gladly wear anything, up to and including a bone through the nose, if only it would help.

Then again, you may recall that one space shuttle was almost recalled when one of the astronauts found himself stricken with — you guessed it — motion sickness. Can't you practically hear this guy saying, "Look, I'll *buy* this shuttle if we can just go home right now."

I can't help wondering if this particular astronaut wasn't the one assigned to KP duty. It seems as if more women than men suffer from seasickness, or are at least willing to admit to it. I've always suspected that this is directly related to the amount of time they spend below decks cooking. If your husband is always standing at the helm thumping his chest while you're down below hugging the head and losing your lunch, maybe you should switch duties for a while. The results might surprise you both.

And finally, even if he turns out to be totally unaffected by the sight of a pair of egg yolks rolling wildly about in imitation of Marty Feldman's eyes, remember this. Somewhere out there is a wave with his name on it. Different seas affect different people. I'm absolutely immune to the effects of the worst pitching, but I've learned to recognize my nemesis, the slow roll brought on by what I can describe only as a long, queasy swell. Other people meet their downfall in the form of a quick, snappy roll. I've yet to meet even a commercial waterman old enough to be over the Captain Macho syndrome who wouldn't admit that there have been times when he's wished that he and his stomach were back on dry land.

So, don't give up. Think positively, and remember that you aren't alone. It's taken me a long time, but I really do believe that I've got this seasickness thing licked. Of course, I still can't read a roadmap in a moving car, but that's a story for another day.

Those Boatyard Blues

One place you'll never see seasickness mentioned is in the yachting magazines. I've often wished that my boating experiences bore some resemblance to the elegant pastime depicted in the advertisements. You've seen how they picture us — nattily-togged, sun-bronzed ladies and gentlemen sipping cocktails and nibbling hors d'oeuvres (prepared by the deck steward, no doubt,) while exchanging *bon mots* about the races at Newport. No one in this world ever trips over the jib sheets, cracks his head on the boom, and calls his very own spouse and young children unprintable names. No one ever feels the first twinge of seasickness. No one is ever shown washing down stale crackers and moldy cheese with warm beer, which might help explain the seasickness. And no boat is ever hauled out except, perhaps, to be loaded as deck cargo to Europe, so no one in these glossy pictures has ever heard of the Boatyard Blues.

That's not exactly the yachting life that I'm familiar with. My style tends more towards paint-spattered blue jeans, outbursts of profanity, Vienna sausages straight from the can, and an endless succession of boatyard haulouts with their accompanying attacks of the Boatyard Blues.

It's not that I don't like boatyards; in fact, I rarely travel anywhere without stopping at every yard along the way. There's nothing like observing what goes on in the average boatyard to restore my faith in mankind's ingenuity, optimisim, and faith. But while a boatyard may be a nice place to visit, I wouldn't want to live in one. Unfortunately, two of my first eight years of living aboard were spent in a yard.

Most of your friends will act as if the Boatyard Blues are contagious. According to the old song, nobody loves you when you're down and out, but according to my observations, they don't love you when your boat's picked up and hauled out, either.

Down and out has its compensations, such as unemployment insurance, food stamps, and leisure time. But when you're up and out, you're on your own. Friends who are forced to drive by the yard on their way to pleasanter destinations speed up and pretend not to notice your forlorn wave. The same people who just happen by the marina every weekend as you cast off the penultimate dockline never happen by the boatyard — ever. Your own family will quickly learn to disappear until after you've loaded the car with tools and supplies and left for the yard. Seasoned owners soon learn to sneak back fifteen minutes later and drag everyone off for a day of enforced labor.

My definition of a friend has thus become simple: A friend is anyone who will come visit you while you're in the yard. A *real* friend shows up wearing painting clothes and brings his own brush. He should also have a soothing repertoire of such phrases as, "It doesn't look that bad to me," "The one on my boat looked much worse but turned out all right," and "I'm sure that it won't cost too much to fix." It doesn't matter if he's lying through his teeth. That's what friends are for.

I was lucky that my friends Chuck and Eloise fit all the above requirements. They came by every day during the wretched nine months I spent on the hill building *Eleuthera* from a bare hull. When the yard that was holding my boat hostage decided, in a frivolous moment, to increase the lay-day fees by six hundred percent, these friends volunteered to help me get the boat in the water — fast.

Eloise and I tackled the bottom painting job. Unlike many novice boatowners who approach this task with more reverence than Michelangelo showed the Sistine Chapel, we had both owned big boats long enough to have adopted a flamboyant, two-handed painting style that got the job done in a hurry. Speed, however, was gained by sacrificing tidiness, and by the time we took our first break, Eloise and I resembled a pair of blue-daubed Picts. Observing us as we sat paint-besmirched on a handy keel block, Chuck promptly broke out with a medley of "Westsails in the sunset, all day I've been blue," followed by a heartening rendition of "Blue, blue, my wife is blue." Neither Eloise nor I found this funny.

The Boatyard Blues can actually cause physical deterioration. Take the great ladder marathon. Even a shallow-draft hull will demand some climbing, and a larger cruiser with a five- or six-foot raft will soon give anyone a case of rubber knees. *Eleuthera*'s railcap was a full ten feet off the ground, and it was another five-foot climb from her cockpit down to the cabin sole. I was younger then, and my knees held out for eight months before the fluid-containing sacs in them ruptured. Although my poor knees sounded, felt, and looked like a pair of rusty hinges encased in water balloons, the building went on for another month before launching brought relief. When I began boating, I'd hoped to develop sea legs; I wound up with boatyard knees instead.

Another common boatyard problem is musical ladders. There are never enough ladders to go around, and unless you can weld a steel ladder to your steel hull, you will eventually find yourself stranded aboard. Shinnying down your anchor line will doubt-lessly put you in the proper frame of mind to deal with the ladder rustlers when you find them. The only method I've found of stopping ladders from disappearing is to pitch such a shrieking,

mouth-foaming fit upon finding the thief that everyone is terrified of the crazy lady on the sailboat. It's embarrassing but effective.

The Boatyard Blues provide no relief from the head hassle, especially if you live aboard. If you can haul and scrub one day, paint and launch the next, this may not bother you too much. When nature calls in the middle of your one night on the hill you merely get up, get dressed, and trudge off to the yard's facilities, assuming that they aren't locked up at night, but the watchdog is. Unfortunately, it's usually the other way around. But this routine quickly palls, especially if you're sharing quarters with small children. Also, most head facilities in boatyards are rather grim. The best make the public restrooms in Central Park look like surgical suites, while the worst should have been burned to the ground by the Board of Health years ago. So I wind up either spurning all liquid refreshments after 6 P.M. or relying on the old bucket-and-chuck-it routine. Do those starry-eyed souls who dream of buying a yacht and sailing off to Tahiti ever consider these seamier aspects of boat owning? I doubt it.

While your friends may make themselves scarce during your haulout, you needn't worry about being lonely. Every yard has its coterie of sidewalk superintendents who love to watch other people work and offer unsolicited advice. We women can expect more than our share, since the average man believes that it is his birthright to know more about boats than any woman.

One day, as I was sanding down *Serenity*'s undercoat, after weeks of smoothing and fairing, I was startled to hear a peremptory voice behind me demand, "What are you doing to that boat?" I did a double-take, making sure that it was my own boat I was working on and not my inquisitor's.

"If you're going to try to do a man's job, you'd better learn to use a man's tools," this particular "expert" informed me. "What you need for that job is a good, big disc sander and some 60-grit discs. That would cut right through that old paint."

I used to waste time and argue with people like that, pointing out that since *Serenity* had just been wooded, there wasn't any old paint left to remove and that a grinder with a coarse disc would cut through her old mahogany planking as well as it cut through paint. But I had discovered that you can't teach a person anything when he thinks that he already knows everything, so I merely flashed this clod a charming smile through clenched teeth and thanked him sweetly for his advice. Thus appeased, he went on his way and I was left to finish my job, by hand.

On this same haulout, I had decided to strip down and varnish *Nity*'s transom, which had been painted a particularly gruesome shade of brown. This had, as usual, turned out to be more of a job than I'd originally bargained for, and I was having endless trouble getting a satisfactory finish coat.

Coat #10 fell victim to a sudden squall, #11 was flattened by the damp night air, #12 was going well until I waved to a passing friend, who pretended, of course, not to see me, and #13 was ruined when a fat blonde in a Cadillac roared through the yard, throwing a non-skid coat of dust and gravel all over the wet varnish. Enraged, I charged into the yard office to complain and discovered just in time that Fatso happened to be the yard owner's wife, the one he'd named his yacht, *Wide Horizons*, after.

Coat #14, at last, looked lucky. The varnish flowed on smoothly and looked as if it was at least six inches deep, as well it might have. I climbed back aboard with a sigh of relief, brewed a cup of coffee, and sat back to gloat over a job that was, finally, well done. Soon my reverie was interrupted by the sound of unfamiliar voices drifting through an open port.

"Don't touch that paint, Harold. It's still wet."

"Oh no, dear," a complacent voice replied. "That's varnish, not paint. Properly done, it always looks wet. See?"

A dismayed duet of "Uh-ohs" confirmed my worst fears. It took me nearly a half hour to get up the nerve to go look. Sure enough, a large, perfect handprint now graced *Serenity*'s formerly flawless stern. My feeling of accomplishment vanished, my plans to launch before the weekend faded, and I felt, once again, those old Boatyard Blues.

Boatyards seem to bring out certain deep instincts in many people. For example, it's impossible for some folks to pass by a hauled-out boat without grabbing its rudder and giving it a swing or two. They usually do this at the precise moment when the boat's owner is in a position either to be thwacked by the tiller or have his fingers fed through a steering sheave. The bigger the rudder, the bigger the temptation: *Eleuthera*'s walloping nine-foot scimitar of an outboard rudder proved so irresistible a temptation that we finally had to clamp a couple of boards on either side of it and bolt it securely in place.

Rudder swingers and hull thumpers are two of a kind. I long ago lost count of the number of times I've stopped what I was doing down below and climbed up on deck to find out why someone was knocking on my hull. The standard conversations I overhear are:

"Wonder what she's made of?"

Thump-thump.

"Guess it's glass."

And "I wonder how thick the hull is."

Thump-thump.

"Sounds pretty heavy to me."

Not all strangers are so easily categorized. The first time I hauled *Syren*, I quickly discovered that she attracted every oddball in Key West, which includes about half the island's population. One hairy, pubescent young man became my particular nemesis. He started out by identifying *Syren* as what he called a "Glou-ces-ter-shire" schooner. Although she did have a saucy sheer, her only resemblance to a Banks schooner lay in her twin spars. I had, by this time, learned to respond to such inane remarks with totally noncommital "ummmms," which usually discouraged any further conversation.

This chap remained undaunted, however, and kept prattling on, even after I stopped responding at all. I thought that I had tuned him completely out when one remark caught my attention,

"You're going to do *what* to your boat?"

"Keelhaul her," he replied smugly.

I knew better than to pursue the matter, but I had to know. "What's that?"

"Well, you run the boat up onto a bank at high water, and then when the tide drops you can scrub and paint."

I knew I should have left well enough alone.

On the other hand, some of my best friends are folks that I first met in boatyards. During this same haulout with *Syren*, I had just managed to get rid of the keelhauler when another fellow wearing leather togs, wrap-around sunglasses, and a ducktail haircut rode up on the biggest motorcycle I'd ever seen. This is not exactly the way your typical wooden-boat enthusiast dresses, so when he strolled over, I was expecting the worst. Uncomfortably aware of this stranger's silent presence at my back, I made a great show of intense concentration on my painting. I was running out of hull to paint and getting more than a little nervous when he finally spoke.

"Excuse me," he said politely. "I didn't want to interrupt you while you were painting, but isn't she a William Garden design?"

It wasn't the first time I've misjudged a person by his appearance, but I was embarrassed all the same. Ken was as mannerly and as knowledgeable as they come, a longtime lover of wooden boats. When I first met him, he was just finishing up a seventeen-foot Wittholz catboat. Later, during all those months I spent working on *Eleuthera*, Catboat Ken would often sail gaily by my shop door on a screaming beam reach and wave, a happy reminder that even for boatbuilders, the Boatyard Blues don't last forever.

One day Eddie, who's in the marine towing and salvage business, called to tell me that he knew of a forty-four-foot steel houseboat being sold for scrap. He mentioned this mainly as a joke; my attempts to make the nautical equivalent of silk purses out of sows' ears were well known. Then again, I'd been living on an eighteen-foot catboat for almost a year and wasn't adverse to the idea of acquiring a larger boat to live on while keeping *Faith* for fun, so I went to take a look.

I've seen some doggy boats in my time, but this one could have been certified by the American Kennel Club. In an initial burst of enthusiasm, the owner had decided to strip off all the old paint. Since he had elected to do this with a grinder, all the protective zinc coating had been stripped off as well. At this point, the owner had developed a terminal case of the Boatyard Blues, which led to his putting the boat up for sale on the hill. Other than some half-hearted painting on the hull, no work had been done in over a year. The hull literally dripped rust, the house was painted a fading, chalky blue, and the decks, to my horror, were covered with bright blue carpet. But the price was *very* right, and, dazzled by the thought of living again with such nearly-forgotten luxuries as refrigeration and hot water, I bought it.

For the first time, I began actually looking at houseboats. I realized that despite a standardized shoebox-on-a-shirtbox basic design, some were decidedly better looking than others and, all things considered, mine wasn't half bad. Then I discovered that the grubby-looking wood that capped *Irish Rose*'s 170-odd feet of metal railing was teak. I immediately began thinking in terms of a dark green hull, buff decks, and varnished teak trim. By the time I recognized the symptoms of what must be a chronic case of the Boatyard Blues, it was too late.

This particular case was aggravated when everyone who passed by my incredible hulk silently assessed her condition, smiled sympathetically, and solicitously inquired, "First boat?"

You would think that launching might provide a cure for this malaise, but sometimes it's more like a final crisis stage. *Syren*'s launch was typical. Since she had no engine, Ecks and I planned to use a dinghy and outboard as a miniature tugboat. The little schooner's seams had opened up considerably while she was up, and I kept her in the lift's slings for a couple of hours while her bottom swelled up tight again. We then started pushing her the half-mile to her permanent berth alongside *Serenity*.

In true double-ender fashion, *Syren* began to squat by the stern and put new areas of open seams under water. I went back to work with the handpump and then, as rising water swirled over my ankles, snatched up a bucket. Noticing our trouble, a friend rowed over in his dinghy and jumped aboard to help. His weight put *Syren* still lower in the water and the sea poured in faster than ever. Blinded by sweat and unable to see where we were, I was about to tell Ecks to beach the boat when *Nity*'s comforting bulk loomed up alongside. I continued bucketing while friends scavenged one of the Matthews bilge pumps and batteries and put them to work.

Soon water was pouring out faster than it was pouring in, and within a few hours, *Syren* had swelled up tight and wasn't leaking a drop. It's too bad that I hadn't had time to keep count, though. I must have set a world record for the number of deep knee bends within a given period, with or without a bucket of salt water. As the old saying goes, there's no bilge pump more efficient than a scared sailor with a bucket.

Serenity herself provided some unwanted excitement on one occasion. We had actually managed to haul and scrub one day, paint and launch the next. Understandably giddy from this unprecedented experience — this had never happened before, and hasn't happened since — I was rash enough to don a fresh white blouse and new white pants in honor of the occasion. Ecks arrived at the yard still wearing his office clothes, and we stood about striking unfamiliar "yachty" poses while the yardbirds launched the boat. We then hopped aboard, kicked over the Ford diesel, and headed for home.

Dressed in our unusually natty attire, sipping cold drinks, and munching on a platter of dainty appetizers, we could, just that once, have posed for one of those yachting ads if *Serenity* hadn't been forty-four years old and a little past her prime for that sort of thing.

As the sun went down, Ecks went aft to strike the ensign. As I rolled the wheel over to port to round a marker, the boat took a deep roll to starboard. Ecks quickly checked the bilges and, never one to rely on understatement when overstatement would do, announced that we were sinking.

Neither of us bothered to roll up our starched white sleeves before diving into the engine room. At least one, and I sometimes suspect all, of *Nity*'s previous owners had drained her engine oil into the bilges, and although I had spent most of a year trying to emulsify the resulting tarry mess, her bilges remained unspeakably vile. However, sinking the entire boat seemed a rather extreme solution, so we groped around in the muck and found the source of the problem, a disintegrated bilge pump hose, by Braille. We quickly replaced the hose and continued on our way.

Thus, our arrival at the yacht club was typical: *Serenity*, as usual, looked like the 1931 Boat Show Queen, while we looked more like oil-rig roustabouts than yacht owners. It occurred to me, not for the first time, that for every year I was taking off my old yacht's apparent age, I was adding at least two to my own.

And then there was *Eleuthera*. Unless you've built your own boat, it's hard to imagine what an emotional experience launching and christening can be. By the time you've reached that stage, your boat represents most of your hopes and dreams, and in my case, my entire net worth. I had planned to make *Eleuthera*'s launch day special, but when the yard got greedy with its lay-day fees, her estimated TUL (time until launching) went abruptly from two months to seventy-two hours. The new yard owners had also declared that I would have to pay again to have them launch her, although I'd already paid the previous owners for this service. My basic philosophy with boatyards is "When in doubt, get her out," and that is what we did.

The new regime was to take over on the first of the month, which also happened to be New Year's Day. Our New Year's Eve was celebrated with bottom paint and resin rather than booze and revelry, and when morning and high tide came, we were ready. The lift operator was a friend who didn't much care whether or not he kept his job, so he joined our conspiracy to get *Eleuthera* into the water and out of the new management's clutches.

Key West is probably never quieter than at 9 A.M. on New Year's Day. The only spectators besides Chuck and Eloise, who had been with us from the beginning, were a few bleary-eyed celebrants who hadn't been able to find their way home yet. I opened a bottle of Mt. Gay rum that we'd saved for the occasion, poured one libation into the Gulf of Mexico for Neptune, and another into a paper cup for the lift operator, who appeared in need of a restorative himself.

I then re-capped the bottle, borrowed a protective leather welder's glove (I'd seen more than one boat launched with equal portions of blood and champagne), and smashed the bottle across *Eleuthera*'s heavy stainless steel bobstay fitting. There was a satisfying shower of rum and shattered glass, and as the heavy sweet fumes drifted on the still morning air, the cutter was lowered slowly away. The scent of the raw alcohol dropped a few of the bystanders much more quickly.

Stepping over these fallen soldiers, we climbed proudly aboard, cranked up the Volvo, and put it in reverse.

Nothing happened.

We gave her some more power.

Still nothing.

I hung over the stern to check the wheel water and realized what was wrong. At peak high water, we were aground in the launching slip.

Never let it be said that bowsprits serve no useful purpose. We gathered up all ambulatory bystanders and herded them out onto the bowsprit, where their combined weight floated *Eleuthera*'s stern free. One trip back to the dock to unload our human ballast, one long blast on the horn, and we were off. I think that members of the New York Yacht Club who screw up christenings this badly are required to turn in their Breton red trousers and commit ritual suicide, but for me, it just seemed natural.

You might think that the Boatyard Blues would be over after the boat has been launched and is safely riding in her slip again, but unless you've been in a boatyard with a "No Cash, No

Splash" policy, the best is yet to come. No matter how much work you've done yourself, the arrival of the bill is almost guaranteed to cause an immediate relapse.

But eventually that shock too will fade, and you'll return to that fool's paradise that we all live in between haulouts. Despite all the evidence and experience to the contrary, I'm still convinced that the next time I haul one of my boats, all she'll need will be an easy scrubbing and a little paint. I even think that I'll have enough money saved to hire most of the scut work done while I relax comfortably at some nearby hostelry and that my Boatyard Blues will be a thing of the past.

I Heard It on
the Radio

If the Boatyard Blues have got you down, it may help to turn on your VHF radio and listen in on some other boatowners' conversations as a reminder that it isn't always fun and games out on the water, either.

Consider the conversations that often develop out of passing situations, although it's not exactly conversation when two irate skippers start exchanging insinuating remarks about one another's ancestry.

The battle lines are clearly drawn between sailors and power-boat operators, with the trawler captains being the nautical equivalent of switch hitters. The same trawler skipper who's cussed out by an angry sailor in the morning may find himself doing some swearing of his own when he's left wallowing in some high-speed boat's wake that afternoon.

A great debate rages over who has the right to be in the Intracoastal Waterway to begin with. You usually hear the sailor's opinion first.

"Hey, Hotshot, if you're in such a hurry, why don't you head offshore?"

Powerboat captains snarl back, "If you blowboats want to sail, why don't you creep along in the ocean and leave the fast lane for us?"

Trawler skippers, chugging along at a stately ten miles an hour, get blasted from both sides.

"Listen, Buddy, if that's a sea-going trawler, why don't you take it to sea and trawl out there?"

As tempers get short, the language becomes more colorful. Eddie and I have been guilty of this ourselves. We were plodding along the Ditch one afternoon when, without any radio call or whistle signals, a big Hatteras suddenly came alongside. Rather late in the game, the uniformed skipper realized that there wasn't enough room to get between our boat and a marker, so he cut across — and almost through — our bow, while simultaneously slowing down to maximum wake which, from a Hatteras, looks like something straight from the Banzai Pipeline. (Our standard joke is that the only time a Hatteras doesn't leave a wake is when it's tied to a dock.)

I was still wrestling with the wheel when Eddie, dodging flying coffee cups, snatched up the mike and asked, "You ever heard of whistle signals, you New York SOB?"

Like most Southern tugboat captains, Eddie uses "New York SOB" as a generic term for any other skipper whose wake knocks him for a loop, but I remember this particular fellow because he grabbed his own mike and indignantly replied, "I'm not from New York!"

When you're the boat which, despite slowing down, has been left doing the Wake Waltz, your VHF outbursts seem totally justified. If, on the other hand, you're merely eavesdropping on other skippers indulging in a name-calling contest, it seems rather childish — and amusing, to a point. But after a while, it can get annoying and once I heard a third skipper, tired of the playground antics of the other two, break in to suggest, "Why don't you two boys pull in to the next marina and slug it out on the dock?"

One radio exchange did end up in physical retaliation. A fellow we'll call Ben was meandering through one of North Carolina's wide sounds in his trawler when a fifty-foot powerboat roared up alongside and plowed past, throwing Ben, his crew, and their lunch in various directions. Adding insult to injury, the powerboat owner made a number of choice remarks over the VHF as well.

A week later Ben saw this same powerboat approaching the marina where his trawler, *Black Duck,* was berthed. Other boat owners watched curiously as Ben, who's in his sixties, staggered down the dock carrying a five-gallon bucket.

He politely introduced himself to the powerboat's owner and asked, "Do you remember me? You passed me in the *Black Duck* back in Albemarle Sound."

The other skipper reluctantly acknowledged this, at which point, Ben announced, "I'm going to do to you exactly what you did to me" and poured his bucket of ice water all over the guy.

While passing situations often lead to skippers' passing remarks, other radio situations can be just as amusing. Last autumn, an otherwise lovely October afternoon was constantly marred by a high-pitched, nasal female voice calling a marina, which was obviously still out of her radio's range. This didn't deter the lady, who kept on calling at increasingly frequent intervals. Nerves began to fray as every minute or two brought her shrill twang back on the air.

In desperation, another voice suggested, "I don't think that marina has a radio."

"Yes, they do," she snapped back authoritatively.

Everyone endured another half hour of audio air pollution before inspiration struck. Claiming to be the marina, another boatowner answered her call and politely accepted her reservations for dockage and dinner that evening. The rest of us silently congratulated this fellow's brilliant maneuver and went our way in blissful silence, with only an occasional twinge of sympathy for the dockhand who would have to tell this formidable woman that no, he didn't have a reservation for her after all.

When the airwaves get busy, confusion is frequently the result.

Another woman was trying to reach a marina and, as soon as she cleared the air, the local marine operator, answering another boat, said, "Shift to channel 24."

"Roger," came the first voice. "24."

Moments later, she was back on 16.

"I can't read you on 24."

The next voice was that of the harbor pilot talking to a ship. "Shift to 18A."

"Roger, shifting to 18A."

This comedy of errors continued through at least a half-dozen "wrong numbers" as this woman snatched numbers off the air and shifted to rather off-beat frequencies, apparently never finding it odd that a different voice was answering her each time. I don't know if she ever talked to the marina or not, since she faded out of my radio range still confused.

When mariners do finally raise a marina, they can ask some interesting questions.

"Which way is the tide running?"

"It's ebbing."

"Yes, but is it ebbing in or ebbing out?"

My favorites are the folks who say, "I'm at marker 64. How long will it take me to reach the marina?"

In what? An eighteen-foot catboat or a thirty-six-foot Magnum?

One night a luxurious marina-resort in South Carolina received a call from a disgruntled customer.

"This is the yacht *Interim* in slip 23."

"Yes, ma'am, how can we help you?"

"If you want to help me, you can do something about the alligator that's in our slip."

(Like what, I wondered. Charge him dockage?)

"I'm sorry, ma'am, but alligators are protected in this state. Is this alligator bothering you?"

"I don't like the way it's looking at my dog, and I want you to do something about it!"

"Yes, ma'am, I'll come try to shoo it away for you."

"Well, you better. I thought this was a nice place to stop, but don't think I'm not going to tell all my friends about *this!*"

Of course, marina workers have their moments, too. If you ask how much depth they have as you approach, the standard answer is an enigmatic "Enough." I know of one marina that has chronic problems with its entrance channel silting up. The owner is very touchy about this, however, so whenever a boat asks how deep the channel is, he cagily asks in reply, "How much water do you need?" Strangely enough, the entrance depth is always exactly six inches more.

But even simple boat-to-boat communications can get complicated when you hear, "This is the powerboat calling the sailboat ahead of me." Sixty sailors' heads swivel about, trying to determine if they're the sailboat in question.

Even the U.S. Navy is guilty of this. Eddie and I were once rambling down the Cooper River in Charleston when we heard a terse voice bark out, "Subtatug."

Subtatug? What the heck was that?

The voice came again.

"Subtatug." That's what we thought he'd said.

We were still puzzling over just what this might mean when the voice gave it a third try.

"SUBMARINE CALLING TUGBOAT UNDER THE COOPER RIVER BRIDGE!"

Oh, *us*. We looked back and sure enough, there was a nuclear submarine slinking along behind our tug. We hustled out of his way.

Few things are more chilling than hearing a "Mayday" cut through the usual radio chatter, but even these sometimes have their lighter side. We listened in on the Coast Guard as they handled one of these.

"What is your position and your problem?"

"We're preparing to abandon ship!"

"What is your position and the nature of your distress?"

"We're hard aground behind marker 43 in the ICW and preparing to abandon!"

"Sir, could you tell me the depth of water at your location?"

"About six inches."

This was the only time I ever heard a Coast Guard radio operator burst out laughing before getting his finger off the mike. We never did find out if this guy abandoned or not, although it's hard to see how he *could* in a half-foot of water.

The Coast Guard is remarkably patient when receiving calls asking for help with seasick crewmembers, spinnaker wraps, and, on one occasion, a whale sighting. The last caller kept insisting that the whale represented a hazard to navigation and that the Coast Guard should do something about it, send out an Ahab, I assume.

A remarkable number of skippers call the Coast Guard for help and, when they're asked for their position, or as the local base usually puts it, their "approximate exact location," they reply, "That's just it. I don't know where I am, and I thought maybe you guys could give me a course back to the sea buoy."

God knows, they try. One radio man, after finally convincing his caller that he didn't really have to say "Mayday" at the beginning of every transmission, kept trying to get some idea of where the boat might be. Finally, in desperation, he asked, "Sir, could you tell me if you remember where it was you *launched* your boat this morning?"

Another group of lost souls thought that their troubles were over when they spotted a freighter which was headed for a nearby port.

"We're all right now, Coast Guard. We've spotted this ship and we're going to follow her into Savannah."

These sailors apparently didn't realize that today's ships clip along at better than twenty-five knots, and it wasn't too long before they were back on the radio with the Coast Guard, complaining, "They wouldn't wait up for us!"

Another jolly crew of drunken fishermen was discovered, well offshore, by the tug *Sea Eagle,* which gave them a heading back to port. The grateful mariners were determined that the tug's captain should receive some fresh fish for his kindness and, ignoring his radio pleas for them to stand clear of the tug and its tow, they maneuvered alongside and tossed the fish aboard.

Moments later, one fisherman's excited voice crackled over the air, "My God, *Sea Eagle,* there's a huge black thing following you!"

Some other folks give their positions in interesting ways. Years ago, a local shrimper achieved lasting fame after breaking down in the Gulf of Mexico. Those were the days before Loran, and by the third night of the search, the stranded shipper was getting desperate. Calling the Coast Guard yet again, he said, "I don't know why you can't find me. I'm right here, right *under* the full moon."

I'd thought that this might be one of those apocryphal stories (about amusing things that always seem to have happened to a friend of a friend) that make the rounds with slight variations throughout the whole country. But not too long ago, I listened to another fellow who'd followed several other boats out to a fishing reef and then made the mistake of not following them home again. Late afternoon found him talking to the marina he'd left that morning, reporting that he was lost. Although the day had been overcast, the western horizon was beginning to clear as the sunset approached.

"Say," the stranded fisherman suddenly asked, "can you see the sun?"

"Yep, it's setting right behind the marina."

"Great, I can see it too! I'll just head right for it and be home in no time!"

(Yes, the Coast Guard finally found him late that night.)

The Coast Guard has a routine set of questions that it asks when problems arise, beginning with a description of the vessel. Sometimes, this seems a bit superfluous. One night, an outright scream of "Mayday" broke through the airwaves. A fifty-eight-foot Hatteras had run onto a set of jetties at full throttle. The radio duty officer was having trouble understanding the skipper, who spoke with a foreign accent. He kept requesting the Hatteras's position, and the captain kept screaming, "On ze rocks! On ze rocks!" Finally, one of the harbor pilots called the Coast Guard and pointed out that a big yacht perched on top of the jetties shouldn't be that hard to spot.

This reminded me of another night when a commercial fishing boat caught fire inside those same jetties. When the Coast Guard asked for a description and position, the owner laconically replied, "You shouldn't have any trouble finding me. I'm the only boat out here that's on fire."

People often wonder about the seemingly inane questions that the Coast Guard asks during emergencies, but often they're just trying to keep the crew distracted and calm. Some radio operators are better at this than others.

"HAVE ALL PERSONNEL DON LIFE JACKETS AT ONCE! Now, what's your documentation number? 540268, gotcha. DOES EVERYONE HAVE HIS JACKET ON NOW? And your hailing port? That's in Maryland, right? JUST HOW FAST ARE YOU TAKING ON WATER? What's the color of your boat's boot stripe? Blue, okay. BY THE WAY YOU DO HAVE A LIFE RAFT ABOARD, I HOPE?"

One skipper, puzzled by the Coast Guard's need to know his wife's maiden name or whatever, asked why the base was asking all these questions. The radio operator, somewhat rattled himself, answered, "Listen, I'm just supposed to keep you talking so you don't panic," which may not have been a particularly comforting thought for the crew.

Even experienced Coast Guardsmen sometimes get a little tongue-tied on the air. One day, a sportfisherman plowed past the base and knocked all the Coast Guard boats for a loop. The radio operator called after the offender and warned him, "You are responsible for your wake. If it has caused us any damage, you will be violated."

Now *there's* a threat for you!

Having amused myself by citing everyone else's mistakes, maybe it's time to confess a few of my own. Because I ran a marina for five years, the local Coast Guard base has learned to recognize my voice. I also presently own several boats — *Irish Rose, Judith R,* and *R.R. Stone,* — which sometimes leads to confusion when I start stumbling, "This is the *R.R. Rose* . . . no wait, make that the *Irish Stone* . . . uh, no that's not right either . . ." only to have the Coast Guard break in with, "Keep trying, you're getting close."

That's bad enough, but it was more embarrassing last summer when we launched our outboard for the first time that season. Although we didn't have any of the Coast Guard-required safety equipment on board yet, we decided to buzz out and visit friends whose boat was anchored nearby. Darkness had fallen by the time we headed for home.

We zipped into the mouth of our creek and then, spotting a forty-one-foot Coast Guard cutter lurking at a dock, chopped the power and started slinking along the opposite bank to avoid detection. The only "safety" item we had on board was my hand-held VHF, which was tuned to channel 68. At that moment, our friends called to see if we'd made it safely home yet.

"No," I whispered. "We're just trying to sneak past the 41396 without being spotted. We don't have any life jackets or lights aboard yet."

Well, the Coast Guard keeps saying they're strapped for funds, but they'd found enough money to buy a scanning VHF. I found this out when my last comments were answered by a cheery Coast Guard voice saying, "We could see that you didn't have lights, Judy, but thanks for telling us about the life jackets."

From now on, I think I'll spend more time listening and less time talking.

Max Wake and Other Nautical Nuisances

The Chatty Patty types who get on the radio and keep on calling until somebody, by God, answers them, are just one variety of character that you get to know along the waterways. Some are more amusing than others, but if you look around your local marina, you'll soon learn to recognize them all.

Most of us have had the misfortune of meeting Max Wake, who's always in a hurry. Max runs at full throttle all day and slows down to full bogging speed only when coming into the marina. Boats already tied up slam against the dock, dinghies are tossed on deck, cocktails crash onto cabin soles, and people changing oil in cramped engine rooms find themselves doing impromptu headstands as Max plows by.

The outraged screams of the boat owners are drowned out when Max picks up his bullhorn to summon the dock crew, as if they didn't already know from the sea of bobbing masts that *something* was coming.

Max's first cousin is Horatio Hornblower. Horatio always calls ahead on VHF and tells the marina crew what time he'll be arriving, but apparently is under the impression that no one who works at a dock is capable of reading a clock. He approaches the dock in one of two ways. Sometimes, he begins blowing his horn at thirty-second intervals while he's still a half-mile away, which is annoying enough. Other times, he waits until he's about five feet away from the dockhand before laying back on his triple air horns. Small attendants are lucky if they're able to grab a piling fast enough to avoid being blown clean off the dock.

Horatio's crew often seem as surprised by the horn as the dock hands. Their motto is "Not Ready When You Are, Gridley," and they continue to sip their drinks and baste themselves with suntan lotion until the boat is two inches away from the dock and Horatio is two seconds away from cardiac arrest before they begin their languid search for lines and fenders.

Faced with this, one captain jumped down from the flying bridge and, while barking orders at this disinterested crew, wrapped a dock piling in a bear hug to secure the boat temporarily until lines were found. Unfortunately, he'd left the engines in gear.

Clinging to his piling, he danced a little jig the length of the cockpit before the boat slid completely out from under him and dragged him over the transom.

Drawn by the loud splash, a crowd of spectators gathered to stare at the jaunty captain's cap that marked the center of a widening ring of concentric ripples. The captain himself soon surfaced, took one look at his amused audience, and spluttered, "It's not funny!" It was, of course, but one dock hand finally stopped laughing long enough to grab a skiff, drag the captain aboard it, and take him out to resume his command, which was still idling down the creek with the crew asking one another, "Where did he say he kept the ropes and bumpers?"

A captain under stress often turns into Ole Yeller, whose voice can be heard long before his boat comes into sight.

"For God's sake, Martha, how many times have I told you how to rig a fender!"

After putting Martha in her place, he starts hollering at the marina crew who, needing no divorce to end the relationship, soon disappear. Sad to say, Ole Yeller doesn't seem to understand why Martha just doesn't enjoy boating the way he does.

A quieter, for fortunately rarer breed is the "Here's Crashing Into You, Kid" captain. A forty-five-foot motorsailer approached the fuel dock where I was working one day at an alarmingly high rate of speed. Instead of hitting reverse, the captain stuck his head out the pilothouse door and announced, "I'm the worst boathandler on the East Coast and I know it, so I always shut the engine down at this point and let the dock crew worry about it." And, to my horror — not to mention the feelings of the owner of the boat in front of him — that's exactly what he did.

Then we have the Committee Boat, which has one captain on the helm and four more on deck who, as the boat nears the dock, make helpful suggestions like, "Faster, Frank," "No, no, slow down!" "Come to port!" "Better make that starboard."

As they tie up, one of the co-captains heaves a line to the dockhand and the others applaud his perfect throw — right in the dockhand's face. Anyone who works at a marina for long eventually finds himself wondering if he has a bull's-eye painted right between his eyes. If not, why do so many people aim their docklines there? The toll in eyeglasses is high, and experienced dockhands have developed a rating scale; lowest points go to the customer who merely dislodges a pair of drugstore sunglasses, while high points are reserved for those who knock a pair of prescription bifocals clean overboard into deep water.

I was working at the marina one day when a sailboat approached the dock with a ten-year-old boy standing on the bow with about a thirty-foot coil of line in his hand.

"Don't throw it yet, Billy," the boy's father cautioned from the helm.

The boat crept closer.

"Not yet."

The boat was practically alongside the dock.

Good, I thought to myself, he's going to get close enough that the kid can just hand me the line.

Therefore, I was standing at ease with my arms folded across my chest when the guy hollered "NOW!" and the kid, with cat-like reflexes, pitched the line at me in a wicked, side-arm throw. The line whipped right around my neck.

"GREAT THROW, BILLY!" his father yelled, apparently failing to notice that I was turning blue.

Another day, the marina's owner and I went to tie up a large, expensive motoryacht. He caught a spring line, and I caught the stern line that was thrown at me by the yacht owner's twelve-year-old son.

"Put that line on that piling, and do it fast!"

I stood there, holding the line and eyeing this kid.

"I *said,* put that line on that piling and do it fast!"

"Put this line on that piling and do it fast, what?"

"Put that line on that piling and do it fast, *now!*"

"Sorry, wrong answer. Let's try it again. Take this line and put it on that piling, *what?*"

"Uh, put it on that piling, please?"

"Why, of course."

I flipped the line over the piling and stared at this little charmer again.

"And what do we say now?"

"Thank you, ma'am."

I don't usually enjoy intimidating children, but in this case, I felt that I was doing the kid a favor. If someone didn't put him straight, he was bound to grow up to be a Prince of Arrogance.

One Prince pulled into the marina and, after I'd tied his boat up, cracked the pilothouse window just enough to tell his uniformed deck hand, "Ask her how much the diesel fuel is." I was standing about three feet away from him at the time, but apparently Princes don't speak to peasants, which tends to make them rather unpopular outside of the immediate royal family.

People like these bother the people who work at marinas, but other characters annoy other customers as well. We've all met the

Sociables, who seem to know everybody.

"Steve! Ethel! Remember us? We tied up behind you in Hope-town. Pull into this slip right next to us!"

Steve and Ethel follow these instructions and, after securing their boat with seventeen docklines, four fender boards, two shore power cords, a water hose, cable TV, and a telephone hookup, learn that they're in someone else's reserved slip.

That doesn't bother the Sociables, who're already holding one of their huge floating cocktail parties in the cockpit. The Sociables' parties run late, but they consider boatowners who turn in early as party-poopers who deserve to be kept awake.

"Hey," Sam Sociable yells at the darkened boat in the next slip, "you want to watch the quiet over there? We're trying to have a party!"

And, alas, their recovery powers are remarkable. Half an hour before daybreak, they're ready to roll again. Sam cranks up his twin turbo 12-71s and revs them for twenty minutes first, while Sue shrieks farewells to friends (and enemies) up and down the dock. When they do finally get underway, Sam gives a final salute with his air horns, just in case they missed anybody.

Mr. Clean also creates problems for other marina guests. Arriving early, he heads directly for the showers. Three hours later, he's still in there doing *something* while the line of would-be washers stretches down the dock. His counterpoint is even worse. No marina crew has ever determined exactly what the Incredible Slob does inside their formerly clean showers to render them unfit for human beings, although washing pigs was one plausible suggestion.

The Earth Family is another crew that's dreaded by marina attendants and customers alike. The Earth Mother's constant refrain is "You kids go play somewhere else while Daddy and I have a drink." Other boatowners are soon reaching for the bottle themselves as her kids play hide-and-seek on a neighboring Huckins and hold contests to see who can run down the dock the fastest while screaming the loudest.

The Earth Mother also loves animals. As her cat, Mizzen, strolls across another boat's galley counter she croons, "Isn't that cute! Mizzen just loves to make new friends!" Earth Mother always owns at least one dog as well, which has been trained to defend its territory so that anyone walking down the dock receives a barking, snarling, growling challenge to his right of passage. People are also forced to dodge canine land mines since the Earth Mother can't bother to see that her dog reaches land in time to relieve itself. She also leaves paper sacks of garbage, including well-used Pampers, on the dock rather than in the marina's trash barrels.

The Earth Father also likes to let it all hang out, literally at times. After a few beers, he decides that there's no need to go below to use the head, when "overboard" is so much nearer. Marina customers and crews alike wish that the entire Earth Family would stay away until they're all toilet trained.

Most people could do without the Salty Old Boatowner, or SOB, too. He's made 432 round trips down the Intracoastal Waterway and wants to tell you about every one of them. He also likes to point out everything that you're doing wrong on your boat, which is everything you're not doing *his* way.

SOBs are usually Helpers. You've already talked to the marina on VHF, and they've recommended you dock starboard side to. As you make your approach, the SOB gallops over to lend an unwanted hand. He yells that you should be coming in portside to and, if you ignore him, he makes great sweeping hand gestures in the apparent belief that you don't understand English. He orders your crew to throw him a bow line instead of the spring line that the dock hand wants, and as soon as he catches it, he hollers, "Don't worry, I've got you!" as he secures it to the nearest cleat. This sends your bow crashing into the dock, at which point the SOB shakes his head and says, "Not a very good landing, son."

Another interesting crew is what we on the East Coast usually refer to as the Lauderdale Lovelies. They invariably arrive on a glittering Magnum that's been custom finished in sixteen shades

of lavender and purple, with coordinated rolled-and-pleated ultra-suede upholstery. I live in a small, sleepy South Carolina fishing village, and an extraterrestrial arriving in a flying saucer wouldn't attract more curious stares than the Lovelies. Their hair is not so much styled as sculpted, with every strand in place despite their boat's forty-knot cruising speed. Each one has at least forty perfectly capped teeth. I've bought cars that cost less than their wrap-around designer sunglasses. Their skins are tanned to a golden brown and glisten with expensive unguents and oils. And there's a lot of skin to glisten, since they all wear embarrassingly tiny bikinis that match their boat. All this glitter is capped off by the shimmering reflections of gold and diamond jewelry that's worth three times my annual income. And these are just the *guys*.

The men who work at the marina are utterly disgusted by these seagoing peacocks. My boss asked one of them, "Does your mother know you run around dressed like this?" and Eddie then commented, as one pranced up the dock, "We always wore more than that *under* our bathing suits." Interestingly enough, I haven't noticed any comments about how disgusting the Lady Lovelies look in their even tinier swim wear.

No one who works at a marina finds Pete and Penny Pincher very amusing, however. The Pinchers rarely cruise in the humble little sailboat you might expect. Instead, they pull in with a boat that cost at least a hundred thousand dollars. They arrive at 6 P.M. during the height of the transient season. They don't want any fuel. They don't want overnight dockage. They just want to walk the dog, use the phone, drop off two weeks' worth of garbage, wash down the boat, take showers, and leave their boat tied up for "Just a few hours" while they borrow the marina's courtesy car and go out for dinner.

When the dockmaster seems less than thrilled by this prospect, the Pinchers tell him that they're retired and living on a fixed income, so they just can't afford dockage. The average dock-hand, who isn't going to be spending the winter in the Caribbean on *his* yacht, is rarely moved to tears by this story, especially since the Pinchers are in their mid-thirties. He also knows that if they do decide to spend the night, they're likely to turn into another disliked customer, the Magician, who ties up and then disappears before paying up.

Sorting the people you meet on the water and around the docks into different categories is fun, but just one thing bothers me. There have been times, I suspect, that I've known them so well because I've fallen into a few of these categories myself.

The Saga of
The Sea Cow

I t's hard to talk about nautical characters without including a certain brand of outboard engine that has a personality all its own.

While reading John Steinbeck's *Long from the Sea of Cortez* the other day, I came across his accurate description of a highly cantankerous British outboard motor whose name he had changed, presumably to protect the guilty, to Sea Cow.

There's simply no middle ground when it comes to Sea Cows. Some folks love them, while others wouldn't have one as a gift. I used to believe that the reason for this dramatically split opinion was that while some folks had never actually owned one of the beasts, they still believed that anything so simple just had to work. Others of us had put this theory to work long enough to know better.

I had originally been a believer in the cult of simplicity myself. Being of a decidedly nonmechanical nature, I thought that the Sea Cow was reassuringly simple in design and construction, with most of its parts right out in the open where you could watch them going about their appointed tasks — most of the time.

This mechanical simplicity appears to be a hallmark of British engineering, which peaked at about the time of Stonehenge and has been gently declining ever since. I should have known better, having cut my teeth on — and clenched them over — those British sports cars of my youth. The English seem to take a perverse pride in the amount of tinkering and puttering necessary to keep one of their mechanical marvels running. Sophisticated engineering, they think, is neither necessary nor desirable: why bother to build a one-piece convertible top when one can simply pull over to the side of the tarmac and spend not much more than fifteen or twenty minutes assembling myriad bits and pieces of metal tubing and then another few moments, not to mention a few fingernails, trying to stretch a stiff hunk of canvas over this flimsy skeleton? So what if you're soaked to the skin in the process? So what if it's stopped raining by the time you've finished? Anyone who's ever owned a British sports car doesn't have any difficulties understanding why the sun set over this particular empire.

To give credit where it is due, however, I should mention that the British are quite sporting about including a very thorough owner's manual with each car. The one for my Austin-Healey was a hard-cover book which was written, alas, in British instead of English. Some words were readily deciphered: "kerb" and "tyre" were self-evident. But after owning this car for seven years, I still wasn't altogether certain just what or where the dashpot flange might be.

A handsome, leather-wrapped tool kit also came with the car, which my father always insisted wasn't a car at all, but rather the missing link between the automobile and the motorcycle. This kit included even a pair of tiny pry bars that looked as if they might be capable of opening a small jar of olives. A careful study of the manual revealed that these were to be used to break the tire off the rim should the need arise. Somehow, I had difficulty picturing myself sitting on the kerb trying to repair my tyre with these little pincers.

A Sea Cow, I am told, comes with just such a manual, complete with basic instructions as to which end of the screwdriver is held in the hand and which is applied to the screw. My Sea Cows (the painful truth is that I owned two before total disillusion set in) came without these manuals, which were doubtlessly heaved overboard by their previous owners in fits of rage after all their careful ministrations came to naught.

The engines I owned revealed another interesting facet of the Sea Cow's character. One had formerly belonged to a fastidious friend (at least, I thought him a friend prior to acquiring this engine), who, after every outing, flushed the engine with fresh water and then oiled and dried it before storing it in its original packing crate until he needed it again. The other engine had belonged to untold numbers of former believers in the simple-has-to-be-better theory and had obviously led a life of less than benign neglect. Oddly enough, the pampered engine wasn't any more dependable than its abused cousin.

In fact, many Sea Cow fans brag that their engines thrive on abuse and cite the experience of John Guzzwell. During his circumnavigation with his twenty-foot sloop, *Trekka*, he broke out his Sea Cow after months of neglect and used it to get through, among other places, the Panama Canal. It worked just fine. I have no reason to doubt this claim, since my own experience with Sea Cows has convinced me that they're simply moody by nature and neither diligent care nor total neglect will ever change them.

My own personal saga of the Sea Cow began as a simple weekend cruise from Key Biscayne to Key West in the twenty-six-foot sloop, *Whisper*. The Sea Cow was not my idea. Ecks and I had chartered the boat to a friend in Miami for six months, and when her venerable old five-horse Johnson had chugged its last, friend Bob had replaced it, in all good faith, with a Sea Cow. He had even gotten the "deluxe" model, the one with a clutch.

Flouting nautical superstition, we began our journey on a Friday afternoon when we boarded a Miami-bound bus in one of Key West's infamous tropical downpours. Although our highway department-yellow foul weather gear didn't look all that unusual, we were also wearing big straw hats and carrying, among other things, a pair of oars, an inflatable raft, binoculars, a hand-bearing compass, and a roll of charts. Our fellow passengers eyed us suspiciously, obviously wondering whether we knew something that they didn't about the safety of the forty-two bridges we would cross before reaching Miami or whether they were about to become unwilling participants in the first bus hijacking to Cuba.

Bob met us at the station, and our plans for an early start were forgotten as we stayed up most of the night swapping sea stories and other lies. I was interested to note how much more plausible Bob's tales of derring-do on the high seas became when they featured my own boat.

As a result, it was the crack of noon before we staggered down to the marina where *Whisper* was patiently waiting, heaved groceries and other gear aboard, and sailed serenely off.

The Sea Cow lounged in a cockpit locker all afternoon as *Whisper* knifed her way south through Biscayne Bay, but sunset and flat calm arrived simultaneously as we reached the shadowing entrance to Jewfish Creek. Ecks yanked a dozen times on the outboard's starter cord before he was rewarded with an ear-shattering "BBRRRIIINNG-A-DING-DING." Oily exhaust fumes billowed from the engine, terrified birds fled from their roosts in the mangroves, and hordes of ravenous mosquitoes erupted from the underbrush. We scrambled about, hastily pulling on long clothes, flailing away at bugs, spraying with 6-12, furling the sails, and digging out the freon horn to signal for the drawbridge ahead of us to open.

Night falls quickly in the tropical Keys, and as we approached the bridge from the Stygian depths of the creek, we could see another sailboat approaching from the other side, which was brightly lit by the lights of two motel-marina complexes. Since we had the current with us — it sometimes seems as if the *only* time the current is ever with us is when we're approaching a bridge — we decided that it would be prudent to signal for an opening a bit sooner than usual. Ecks hoisted the freon horn overhead, aimed it at the bridge tender's house, and, as we braced ourselves against the expected barrage of noise, hit the button.

"Phhfffttt."

In a rare burst of planning and efficiency, we had purchased a new freon cannister just for this trip. It was a dud.

I grabbed the old brass mouth horn from its accustomed rack just inside the companionway and gave the old three-blast bridge-opening signal.

"FLLAAAHHHNNNNT."

"FLAAHhnnt."

"Flah."

A three-pack-a-day nicotine habit hadn't provided very good training for blowing a horn, and the warning that cigarette smoking might prove hazardous to one's health took on new meaning as the current swept *Whisper* on towards the bridge.

But to our immense relief, the bridge opened, and trailing our cloud of smoke, fumes, bugs, and noise, we proceeded on our way. The boat approaching us passed under the bridge first, and then, despite our frantically repeated horn blowing, spotlight waving, and shouting, the bridge began to close. Since there was neither time nor room to anchor, our only hope lay in spinning about 180° before the two closing spans clamped shut on *Whisper*'s mast.

It was at that precise moment that the Sea Cow chose to quit.

The most charitable assumption that I can make is that it fainted from sheer terror. In the sudden silence that I was soon to know well, I held my breath for the long moment it took *Whisper* to drift under the jaws of the bridge, which snicked shut just behind her spar.

Feeling immeasurably older and tireder than we had on the other side of the bridge, we drifted alongside a Chris-Craft whose owner graciously accepted the inevitable and invited us to tie up alongside overnight. Equally gracious, I refrained for once from offering my unsolicited opinion of power boats in general and Chris-Crafts in particular. As a punishment for its inexcusable and inexplicable dereliction of duty, the Sea Cow was ostracized for the remainder of the evening. We would look for the source of its trouble in the morning.

Once *Whisper* was safe and secure, we realized that the mosquitoes had brought in reinforcements while we were distracted and that the cabin was now resonating with their high-pitched, hungry whine. We lit four citronella candles, sprayed from head to toe with all three brands of mosquito repellent on board, and, choking in the resultant fog, lamented the lack of our old standby, Pic coils. We searched the entire boat for the screens that had been on board when *Whisper*'s charter began and finally decided that Bob must have lost them. (As often happens on my boats, they mysteriously reappeared in the forepeak months later.)

Finally, we each wrapped up in the sail of our choice, the bed linens having disappeared also, and stretched out on the sticky vinyl-covered berths. Basting in sweat and bug spray, tingling with wind and sun burn, and smothering in expensive Dacron, we spent most of a sleepless night cursing Bob, whom we envisioned sleeping peacefully in air-conditioned, insect-free comfort.

Still awake at four, we both crawled out in the cockpit.

"We've got to get some sleep," Ecks hissed over the mosquitoes' maddening drone. "Maybe we'd better give up and rent a room in the motel."

"Don't bother," came a weary voice from the Chris-Craft next door. "Its rooms are full of bugs, too."

At daybreak, after trying to revive ourselves with hot coffee and cold showers, we marched back on board, flung open the lazarette, and awakened the faithless Sea Cow with a vicious yank on the starter cord.

"BBRRRIINNNNG-A-DING-DING!"

Apparently anxious to make up for the previous night's display of nerves, the engine started, for once, on the first try. With a silent apology to our neighbors, who couldn't have heard a spoken word over the Sea Cow's bark, we motored thoughtfully on our way.

Although we were hardly in any condition to appreciate it, the day was a fine example of the Keys weather at its best. The temperature was in the low 80s, the sky was azure blue, and the warm sunlight reflected off the white sand bottom to create constantly changing patterns of neon blue and iridescent green. However, as the sun rose higher, the wind increased rapidly, and when we came to a sharp dogleg to windward, Ecks rolled a deep reef in the mainsail, which promptly drooped and sagged into its well-known imitation of a well-used potato sack. The sloop's roller reefing system left much to be desired. Also, the smallest headsail was the alleged "working" jib, which was still too big for the amount of wind we were suddenly facing.

While we were debating whether or not to tackle this stretch under sail or take our chances with the Sea Cow again, a sports-fisherman stopped to watch the show, and naturally, our sailors' egos demanded that we sail blithely on. *Whisper* heeled down and shouldered her way through the choppy water, reaching her mark in only two tacks. We waved casually to the fisherman, making it obvious that we'd never had any doubts.

Even our doubts about the moody Sea Cow were forgotten as *Whisper* fell off on a close reach and raced her own shadow across the bottom. The route from Jewfish Creek to Marathon cut across the shallow, open sounds and bays that make up Florida Bay and was interconnected by either natural tidal creeks through the dense mangroves or man-made cuts dynamited through coral. Whenever *Whisper* entered a mangrove cut, she would suddenly lurch upright, practically becalmed in the lee of the thick trees. Ghosting through and barely maintaining steerageway, we slid silently past groups of small anchored boats whose occupants sported at least five fishing poles apiece, making their boats resemble brightly-colored sea-going porcupines.

In one cut, a large houseboat unexpectedly upped anchor and backed across our bow, nearly blocking the channel. Ecks jumped to the lazarette and tried to start the Sea Cow so we could clear this new obstacle. His efforts produced nothing but a startled cough, and by the time the starter cord was re-wound — Sea Cows, you understand, have not yet succumbed to decadent American luxuries like automatic rewinds — we had squeaked under the houseboat's stern under sail.

We exchanged suitable remarks regarding seamanship and ancestry with the houseboat's crew and then, honor thus upheld on both sides, went our separate ways. I noted, not for the first time, that while the surprises and vicissitudes of a sailor's life offer superb training for the sort of verbal pyrotechnics these situations require, powerboats do have a decided edge when it comes to leaving in an indignant huff. It's hard to convey an adequate impression of righteous indignation when you're barely drifting away.

Moments later, we were in the clear again and small boats scattered out of the channel like wind-blown leaves as *Whisper*, with thirty knots of wind in her sails and a white bone in her teeth, suddenly heeled down and charged into their mist. Thus the afternoon passed.

Although Lower Matecumbe Harbor was ominously marked "Abandoned" on our chart, there were both a marina, where we tied up overnight, and an anchorage, which backed onto busy U.S. Highway 1. The wind whistled and shrieked through the rigging all night, keeping the temperature down and the mosquitoes grounded.

We had both collapsed after dinner and remained oblivious to the outside world until the next morning, which started with a literal bang when a twenty-two-footer with twin outboards ricocheted off *Whisper*'s flank while aiming for the gas pumps a full hundred feet down the dock. This certainly helped get the old adrenalin flowing early, but since the wind was also showing signs of increasing vigor, we decided that we'd better anchor the sloop out and return to Key West by bus in order to make it back to work on time. The owner of a nearby trawler yacht joined me on the dock as Ecks coaxed the Sea Cow into starting.

"I've heard some good things about those Sea Cow engines.

How do you like yours?"

"I don't."

I flipped the dock lines to Ecks and warily eyed some old concrete pilings that *Whisper* would have to skim past.

"It seems to run well enough," my new-found friend bellowed over the din of the engine. "What is it that you don't like about it?"

His shouted question rang out in the deep silence that fell as the Sea Cow quit. *Whisper* was, of course, directly upwind of the pilings and making rapid leeway towards their jagged reinforcing bars. The silence was quickly filled with Ecks's mellifluent cursing, and my friend, nodding slowly, was clearly beginning to see my point. On this occasion, Irish temper overcame English obstinacy, the Sea Cow recovered rapidly from its swoon, and *Whisper*, unscathed, slid out to the anchorage.

"Does it stop like that very often?" my companion asked.

"No," I sighed. "Only when you really need it." We went to flag down the bus.

"Didn't get very far," our driver pointed out, as if we hadn't noticed this ourselves.

One norther after another swept the Keys as we waited in Key West for better weather. Finally, the forecast called for winds of fifteen to twenty knots and, worried about leaving the little sloop unattended any longer, we decided to sail.

"See you again soon," our driver called optimistically as he dropped us off in the dark. Ecks rowed out to *Whisper*, started the reluctant engine, and hoisted the small anchor. The big kedge, however, was clinging to the bottom with a tenacity that would have been admirable under other circumstances. The wind moaned, a chill rain began to fall, the Sea Cow bring-a-ding-dinged, and still Ecks heaved on the anchor.

This sort of exercise can be quite amusing when viewed from a distance, and a small crowd had gathered on the dock to watch. Eventually we saw the anchor break the surface, still grasping a large chunk of reinforced concrete which it reluctantly released and allowed to fall back into the water.

Ecks had just reached the cockpit when the Sea Cow, with its customary flair for timing, quit. As the wind skidded *Whisper* backwards towards the viaduct on U.S. 1, he sprinted back to the bow without breaking stride and heaved the kedge back overboard with a truly vile oath that would have shocked Neptune himself. His dockside audience responded with spontaneous whistles and applause. Operating on the theory that discretion is indeed the better part of valor, Ecks rowed in to collect me and the groceries, and we spent the night at anchor.

The morning weather forecast was deceptively promising, offering the hope of easterly winds at only fifteen knots. The Sea Cow, which always seemed braver by daylight, ran docilely enough, but we kept the main and jib ready to hoist anyway and hugged the windward side of the channel leading out of the harbor, just in case. Sure enough, the Sea Cow quit again, but this time we were ready and had *Whisper* under sail in seconds. I triumphantly slammed the hatch on the sulking engine and we proceeded on our way.

As soon as we were committed to our downwind course, the wind again began to howl and soon *Whisper* was surging along with just her deep-reefed main pulling her through the foam-flecked bottle-green water. There was no way we could beat our way back into the wind, so we pressed on to Marathon.

As we entered Bayles Boatyard, we would be on a close reach in over thirty knots of wind with an interesting assortment of power lines to leeward, so we decided that the time had come to reason with the engine. Our situation was explained to the Sea Cow in great detail, the need for cooperation was stressed, and I believe that some mention was made of an instant watery grave should it fail us this time.

This little pep talk seemed to help. The Sea Cow started promptly and ran enthusiastically as we sailed the length of the channel. It continued to run as we shot up into the wind and stopped, bow precisely six inches from the dock, gunwales precisely six inches from the finger pier. It continued to run while we walked to the store, and it was still running when we returned.

It ran no matter what we did, including slamming the hatch on it in the sincere hope that it would strangle on its own exhaust fumes. Our frustration with the Sea Cow reached new heights: we had never even put the unreliable beast into gear and now it sat, brring-a-ding-dinging proudly and taking all the credit for *Whisper*'s flawless approach and landing.

This time the Sea Cow joined us on the bus back to Key West. Although we had already dismantled it several times without discovering the source of its malaise, we called in a friend who had a way with outboards for a second opinion. He couldn't find anything wrong with it either, and of course, it ran perfectly in the test tank. We all finally agreed that its problem must by psychosomatic. However, we didn't have any other engine to take its place, so we lugged the faithless Sea Cow back to Marathon with us the following weekend. Our regular bus driver was off, but his replacement, who had obviously been told of our by-land-and-by-sea journey, promised to keep an eye out for us Sunday.

But this time he was wrong, and the final leg to Key West was a joy. The wind was easterly again, but this time it held steady at fifteen to eighteen knots. Backing the jib, we backed *Whisper* out of her slip and into the channel, then across the flats of Florida Bay and out Moser Channel through the Seven Mile Bridge. Once in the relatively deep water of Hawk Channel, we swung downwind and set our course for home.

Running inside the Key's protective living coral reef, Hawk Channel provides great sailing. To the north, a long emerald necklace of keys strung together with a fragile tracery of bridges forms the horizon. To the south lies a series of lights marking the outer reef, and a steady parade of freighters either rides the Gulf Stream to the east or slips westward just inside its flow.

With her mainsail guyed out to port and her big Genoa poled out to starboard, the little gray sloop rolled along, lifting occasionally to a following sea and surfing briefly along its face. The water was pure turquoise and so clear that we could see starfish clutching the bottom twenty feet below us. We snapped on the radio for a weather report and picked up Harry Belafonte singing calypso instead. Warm sunshine, a cool breeze, lilting island music, and a good boat: every now and then, everything falls into place and you remember why you got hooked on boating in the first place.

This was the best day of the trip for another reason. The Sea Cow was exiled to the cockpit locker for the entire day. When *Whisper* reached her berth in Key West, we threw the Sea Cow on the dock and left it there. We had decided that sailing with no engine at all was preferable to sailing with one that we couldn't count on, an opinion that still stands. For the rest of the time that we owned *Whisper*, we relied on her good sails to get us where we were going and her good ground tackle to keep us away from any trouble we couldn't escape under sail. We took pleasure in working the sloop in and out of tight places, playing currents and counter-currents, and gliding silently home at dusk on night breezes that seemed to exist only in *Whisper*'s imagination.

It's been many years since I've had a Sea Cow on any of my boats, but every now and then someone notices the little two-horse outboard on my dinghy and asks if I've ever considered using one of those wonderful Sea Cow outboards instead. Then, like the Ancient Mariner, I fix my listener with a gimlet eye and tell, once again, the Saga of the Sea Cow.

As a matter of fact, a few years ago I told this story in the pages of a national boating magazine. In an effort to avoid hurt feelings, not to mention lawsuits, I had followed Steinbeck's lead and used the Sea Cow name. Editors are a wary lot, however, and I had some trouble selling the story even after providing the guilty party with an alias. I finally pointed out that, short of fire-bombing the manufacturer, there was no way that I could cause the Sea Cow people any more trouble than they had already caused me.

At the same time, I warned the editor that he would most likely be hearing from other owners of this same brand of engine who would claim for it such virtues of reliability, dependability, and loyalty to its owner as would put Lassie to shame.

Sure enough, a number of the magazine's readers leapt to their typewriters — or, perhaps, given their penchant for simplicity, their quill pens — to defend the Sea Cow. The manufacturer, who either enjoys a typically British sense of humor or knows the truth when he sees it, held his peace.

One gentleman, convinced that I was mistaken about the true identity of Steinbeck's original Sea Cow, asked huffily if I had ever heard of the Johnson Sea Horse. As a matter of fact, I own two Sea Horses right now and have nothing but praise for them. They're appropriately named, since they remind me of a pair of old, dependable work horses; strong, quiet, and reliable, they have yet to fail me.

That got me to thinking about names, and for the first time I realized how accurately the Sea Cow, better known as the Sea Gull, was titled. Like their airborne namesakes, they're dirty, loud, and noisome.

Another member of the Loyal Order of Sea Gulls took me to task for implying that these engines are perhaps a bit noisier than necessary. Well, "loud" is, of course, a subjective term. I spend a fair amount of time aboard a steel tugboat whose 16-71 GM diesel, accompanied by a mechanical chorus of generators, air compressors, and pumps, screams mightily in a vast, resonating engine room. There's no room for debate here: it's loud. At the same time, it's producing vast amounts of horsepower and moving considerable tonnage through the water.

Both of my Sea Gulls shrieked but a few decibels lower while moving infinitely less boat through the water. On a scale of one to ten, with one being the silence of eternity and ten being the sound of the universe being created in the big-bang theory of creation, I'd rate the average Sea Gull at about an eight.

I've often wished that I'd paid more attention in my statistics class so I could do some research on the divorce rate among Sea

Gull owners. (Passing the course would have been nice, too.) It isn't so much of a problem when you're underway, since the Sea Gull's jackhammer tones eliminate all possibility of conversation, including counter-productive remarks like, "I *told* you that we should have bought an Evinrude." But at docking time, when teamwork and communication become important, the Sea Cow will tax the patience of the most compatible couple.

I had had more than ample opportunities to experience this at first hand while sharing *Whisper* with a Sea Cow, and had not been amused. However, the day after I sold her, I had the chance to be the amused audience as her new owners approached the slip next to mine.

"How close are we to the dock?" Allen bellowed over the merry bring-a-ding-ding of the Sea Cow.

I could see his wife Elaine's lips moving in response.

"WHAT?"

Her lips moved again.

"How in the hell am I supposed to hear you? Speak up!"

"Why are you yelling at me? I've answered you twice already!"

"WHAT? WHAT?"

"SHUT UP!"

It was easy for me to recognize the old familiar Sea Cow syndrome. Whoever is sitting by the engine yells to be heard over its roar, while the person standing in the relative quiet of the bow can't understand what all the hollering is about and replies in normal tones — for a while. By the time the engine is finally shut off, the silence is truly total, since no one is on speaking terms any more.

The day after this episode, Allen bought a U.S.-built outboard and advertised the Sea Cow in the local paper, which brings to mind another interesting point. Ever notice how many Sea Cows are listed for sale with the comment "Only used once"?

Another letters-to-the-editor writer protested that U.S. outboards are "junked up" with fancy covers and hoods that "make it difficult to locate the outboard." True enough, I never had any trouble locating my Sea Cows: I just followed my nose and my ears and found them every time. But I can't say as I've found my Johnsons very elusive, either. And while the notion of having everything "right out in the open" may sound appealing when you've got to work on the engine, you're a lot less likely to have to work on it in the first place if everything is neatly tucked under a cover and out of the salt spray. After all, the average surgeon would probably find it easier to work on your appendix if it were right out in the open, too, but there are good reasons Mother Nature didn't design us that way.

The same chap reported indignantly that *his* Sea Cow never gave him any trouble, although he had used it for a couple of "long runs," of eight and nine miles, respectively. Now, admittedly, eight or nine miles in the raucous company of a Sea Cow *seems* like a voyage of epic proportions, but most of us expect our engines to run eight or nine years, not miles.

Finally, an otherwise sensible friend took me to task for maligning his favorite engine and asked somewhat plaintively if I couldn't find any redeeming virtues in the Sea Cow. After much thought, I came up with two good points.

First, the Sea Cow feeds on an extremely oil-rich fuel, which allows it to emit great greasy palls of smoke. Small boats are always concerned about being seen by larger vessels, but a Sea Cow-propelled craft can be spotted long before its mast ever breaks over the horizon by this plume of blue-gray smog. Closer to shore, this same smoke screen lays down an effective fog against mosquitoes, while the noise of the engine drowns out the otherwise distressing sound of millions of bugs coughing their little lungs out.

I'm surprised that none of the Sea Cow fans, who tend to be into earth shoes, backpacking, brown rice, and living off the land, mentioned the other feature of this engine that is unique. The old Sea Cow's big four-bladed, square-tipped wheel made it a devastatingly effective harvester of sea weed. It even let you know when it was time to harvest your crop by bogging down and then stopping completely. Kelp *au gratin*, anyone?

Even allowing for these dubious advantages, I still have trouble explaining the differences of opinion on these engines. No one is neutral. I've finally reached the conclusion that it's the familiar "lemon" theory in reverse. We all know that even the most reliable manufacturers occasionally turn out a product that seems haunted by gremlins and never works right. It seems to me that the people who build the Sea Cow sometimes have just the same sort of fluke with the opposite result and come up with an engine that we shall call a "plum." This Sea Cow starts easily and reliably, runs smoothly, doesn't belch out clouds of smoke that make your boat resemble a sea-going version of Pittsburgh, and doesn't stop until you want it to.

That's my theory, anyway. But the people who maintain that the Sea Cow is the finest engine in the world (a modest claim which the manufacturers themselves emblazon on their engines) are just as entitled to their erroneous belief as those of us who regard it as the foulest and know that its black paint job hides an equally black heart.

The Battle of the Bridge

I was probably still thinking about the time that the swooning Sea Cow almost allowed *Whisper*'s mast to be bitten in half by a closing bridge when a group of boatowners got talking about their favorite boat-related movies the other day. Several mentioned *Dove,* another opted for *The Sea Wolf,* and some classicists cited either *Mutiny on the Bounty* or *Captain Courageous.* After everyone else had made his selection, I announced mine: *The Bridge on the River Kwai.*

"That's not a *boating* movie!"

"What about the scene where they blow up the bridge? Anyone who's ever cruised the Intracoastal Waterway would have to consider that one of boating's finer moments."

As far as I'm concerned, boats and bridges are natural enemies, and although the odds in any dispute are overwhelmingly on the side of the bridge, boatowners still continue to do battle like water-borne Don Quixotes tilting at windmills. This is particularly true along the bridge-infested ICW.

Until relatively recent years, none of the Waterway's bridges was radio equipped, and all communications were made with horns. Many bridges still rely on whistle signals, and although this system of communications works well in theory, in practice it sometimes leaves something to be desired — like the bridge's opening when you want it to. In fact, many boatowners firmly believe that the one requirement for becoming a bridge tender is total deafness.

The scenario is too familiar to Waterway veterans. You've studied the latest edition of the *Waterway Guide,* which struggles valiantly to keep up with the ever-changing bridge restrictions, and it has assured you that this bridge will open on demand. You steam confidently up to it and blow your horn.

And then you wait. No answer from the bridge. You keep on coming and hit the horns again. Still nothing. You realize that a favorable current, the first you've encountered since the last bridge, is sweeping you down towards the unyielding span at an alarmingly rapid rate.

You stick your head out the pilothouse window and listen for the warning bells that indicate that the roadway gates are about to drop. No bells. You look for the flashing lights that warn oncoming vehicles to stop. No lights. You peer into the bridge tender's house through the binoculars for signs of life. Nothing. Your nerves can't take it any more, so you spin into a 180° turn.

The moment that you're broadside to the bridge, things begin to happen. Lights. Bells. Action. You gun your boat through its turn and start swinging back towards the bridge again. By the time you're lined up, the bells have stopped clanging. The lights have stopped flashing. The barriers are back down. The tender has disappeared. You spin into another turn.

This is known as the Waterway Pas de Deux, and the dance may be repeated until the boatowner gives what some tenders regard as the proper signal: horn blasts accompanied by the skipper's screaming until the cords in his neck stand out as he throws his hat down on the cockpit sole and jumps up and down on it. At this point, the tender may go ahead and open the bridge. But when you do finally manage to fling your boat through the bridge before he changes his mind again, the tender is likely to hang out his window and drawl, "Why can't you guys make up your minds?"

What the skipper replies shall go unprinted.

If it's any consolation, some daring bridge tenders even perform this ballet with oncoming tugs and tows, which sometimes find themselves sprawled gracelessly alongside the bridge and its fender system before it's all over. On the other hand, tugs do occasionally win this war of nerves by plowing into the bridge and knocking it down, tender's house and all.

All of this, of course, depends on your giving the right signal to begin with. A while back, Eddie and I were bearing down on a radio-free bridge with our forty-seven-foot tug, *R.R. Stone,* and a dredge in tow. Over the years, separately and together, we had opened thousands of bridges with the old three-blast signal.

I was on the wheel as we approached when I suddenly remembered that this opening signal had been changed so that it wouldn't be confused with the signal meaning "My engines are going astern," although by the second time you signalled, this was as often as not the case. (Not when you have a barge in tow, of course, since going astern then means that you will (a) catch the towing hawser in the wheel or (b) back into your own tow or (c) both of the above.)

What I couldn't remember was just what the new signal might be. Therefore, I cunningly slapped one hand over my eye and exclaimed, "Ouch, I've got something under my contact lens," while handing the wheel over to Eddie.

He had been running boats for a living while I was literally still in diapers, and he isn't too inclined to ask for my advice on nautical matters. He also takes any changes in the Rules of the Road as a personal insult, blaming them on the same people who tried to force the decimal system on him. I was curious to see what he would do.

We were uncomfortably close to the bridge, which was obviously oblivious to our existence, before he grudgingly asked,

"All right, what the heck is the opening signal any more?" Actually, he said quite a bit more than that, but I thought that a bit of editing might be advisable.

The long and the short of it was that, although I couldn't remember it at the time, a long and a short blast was what was needed. Instead, we gave a couple of rather indeterminate blasts and hoped for the best. Fortunately, the bridge tender that night wasn't the sort who sits and stares at you until, by God, you give the *proper* signal.

At least with a tug and a tow you know that the bridge is legally required to open for you. As more and more bridges add restrictions to their opening hours, life afloat gets more interesting. Some districts are sporting enough to put up a sign announcing the bridge schedule a half-mile before the bridge itself, and they use lettering large enough to be read without your running aground while trying to get close enough to decipher the rules.

In other areas, however, signs are nailed to the bridges themselves and printed in the same size type as the phone book. This means that you've usually been swept into the fender system by the inevitable favoring current before you can spell out the regulations:

"Bridge opens every half hour between 6 and 7 A.M. Bridge will not open between 7 and 9 A.M. After 9 A.M., bridge opens every hour on the three-quarter hour until noon. From noon to 1 P.M., bridge opens only for red north-bound vessels. On alternate Fridays that are even-numbered national holidays, the Governor's birthday, and days containing the letter *R*, bridge opens only for vessels with more than 6 persons on board."

After you've spent ten minutes interpreting this sign, you realize that you've just missed the last opening by two minutes, and now you're going to have to wait another hour unless, of course, they change the rules again in the meantime.

The tidal boards that are supposed to give the bridge's exact clearance are another good idea that may or may not work. First, by the time you're close enough to read the board, it's marginal whether or not you can back out from under the bridge if you *can't* clear it. And it's always interesting to learn at the last moment that the critical lower numbers on the board are illegible. The final problem, of course, is knowing your own boat's clearance.

Some modern boatbuilders do give new owners their boats' exact clearance, but that's before you start adding radars, antennas, and all the other expensive goodies that lower your clearance and raise your repair bill if you guess wrong.

Serenity's former owner had carefully logged her different clearances with various masts and antennas up or down. Ecks and I promptly started changing things, including adding a new VHF radio to supplement her double sideband rig, which was still legal back then and which sported a twenty-four-foot antenna. Since we were in a hurry to try out this new radio, we rather inelegantly secured its six-foot antenna to the air horns, lashing it in place with marline. (This temporary installation was still in place when we sold her two years later.) Then, without checking our altered bridge clearance, we set off for a weekend in Marathon in the Florida Keys.

We decided to circumnavigate Boot Key, which meant passing through a bridge with limited clearance. We thought that we could clear it without opening the bridge or dropping the new antenna, but Ecks wanted me to stand outside the pilothouse door and eyeball it, just to be sure. I was peering back and forth from the VHF antenna to the bridge when I heard someone hail me.

It was the bridge tender, who genially pointed out, "That little antenna's gonna clear just fine, but ain't no way that big one will." While concentrating on the VHF, we had totally forgotten the big double-sideband rig, although I was standing right in front of it. We backed clear in time to avoid any damage, but the next day we took a short cut under the old Seven Mile Bridge, where the clearance was even lower. We had usual current boiling along with us, so we were approaching at a fast clip. We were about ten feet away from the bridge when I stuck my head out the pilothouse door and immediately snatched it back in, yelling "Yipes!" Ecks didn't have time to ask me what was wrong before we heard the big antenna slam into the bridge and girders with a metallic "Ta-whocketa-whocketa-whock!" To our amazement, the antenna was still with us on the other side. However, since we were surrounded by an audience of other boats, we had to look nonchalant, as if we ran twenty-four-foot antennas under fifteen-foot bridges all the time, which wasn't so far from the truth by then.

Over the years, improvements have been made on the ICW's bridges. For one thing, there aren't any more bridges where the tender does double-duty as a toll collector. Trying to get one of these to open was always good for a thirty-point increase in the most phlegmatic sailor's blood pressure. The increasing use of VHF radios on bridges has also helped matters, at least when the tender hasn't turned his off so he can watch the television without interruption.

The *Waterway Guide* cheerfully notes that radio-equipped bridges "may not have time to answer you" but will "probably" open anyway. Forgive me if I'm wrong, but I thought that the whole point of this exercise was that you would *know* when and if a bridge would open. After all, how long does it take to pick up the mike and answer an oncoming boat?

But no, the familiar *pas de deux* continues, although a little more coordination is now required of the skipper who has to steer in circles, blow his horn, and yell into the radio at the same time. If he perseveres long enough, a bored voice may finally reply, inevitably saying, "Keep her comin', Cap," which is hard to do when the road traffic seems to keep on coming, too.

Even if you do establish communication, problems may still arise. Eddie and I once found ourselves delivering a forty-seven-foot yawl with a sixty-five-foot mainmast south. To make matters more interesting, we had a thirty-four-foot sailboat in tow for a while. One blustery December afternoon found us approaching a swing bridge in forty-knot winds. Much to our relief, our radio call was quickly answered by a female tender, who promised us an opening. We were still a half-mile north of the bridge and making slow progress.

As we neared the span, we began anxiously eyeing the traffic. Nothing happened, although we did notice a couple of pedestrians on the bridge. Finally, we were too close to ignore the situation any longer, and we called the bridge again.

"Hey, are you going to open for us or not?"

"Where are you, Cap?" a male voice replied.

"Right on top of you, for God's sake!"

Obviously, the first tender hadn't bothered passing our message along to her relief, nor had he thought to look out the window. So much for total reliance on VHF.

But when we approached the Thunderbolt Bridge in Georgia, this time without our tow, we tried again. A tugboat and another sailboat would pass through the bridge first, so we called and asked if the bridge could hold the opening for us.

"We're the third boat in line, a forty-seven-foot white yawl with a sixty-five-foot mainmast."

"Keep her comin', Cap."

The bridge was a fast one, opening smartly. To avoid tying up traffic any longer than necessary, we hooked up the yawl and, with a boost from the current, approached the bridge at ten knots.

The tug went through. The first sailboat went through. And then a tiny blue sailboat zipped out from a nearby marina and scooted under the bridge. We called again.

"Yawl *Chantecler* here again, Thunderbolt."

"Keep her comin', Cap. I gotcha."

He almost got us, all right. We were zooming into the fender system when the spans began to drop.

Now Eddie, who's worked boats for a living all his life, subscribes to the commercial waterman's creed: No matter what happens, you stay cool on the radio. This was the only time I ever heard him speak in anything other than a laid-back drawl.

"WHOA, THUNDERBOLT!"

The bridge tender might not have been able to count, but there was nothing wrong with his reflexes. The spans screeched to a stop and then began to lift again. We made it through with both masts still intact, but to this day Eddie denies saying anything so un-nautical as "Whoa" on the VHF and claims instead to have said, "Say there, Thunderbolt, you want to hold it for a minute?" But I know better.

A friend was less fortunate. He had also followed another boat through an open bridge, only to have the closing spans clamp down on his formerly deck-stepped mast. After re-stepping the mast on the keel, the bridge continued to force the boat under-water until the spans were closed.

Shouting didn't do any good, so Al climbed into his dinghy, rowed over to the fender system, climbed it, and went into the tender's house. Dripping wet, he asked, "Did you see a green sloop go under the bridge a couple of minutes ago?"

"Sure did."

"Well, did you ever see it come *out* again?" Al demanded, pointing a quivering finger at the splintered stub of varnished spruce that stuck up in the roadway.

"Son of a gun" is all the tender is reported to have said, although I doubt that Al gave him enough time to say even that much.

Admittedly, the problems don't all lie with the tenders: no matter what they do, someone's going to be mad with them. But sometimes, they get to have a laugh on us.

Several summers ago, we were heading south on our sixty-five-foot tug, *Judith R*, with a forty-five-foot tug in tow. We were hot, we were tired after six twenty-four-hour days of non-stop towing, and, since the cook, who shall remain nameless, had miscalculated the supplies, we were getting rather hungry as well. Tempers were getting short — in other words, a typical tow.

The watch had just changed, and the wheelman told Eddie that we were approaching the Figure Eight Island Bridge. We rambled along and soon spotted the bridge. Eddie gave them a call.

"I can't see you yet, Cap."

"I'm southbound."

"I *still* can't see you."

"Look, I'm a 65-foot red tug towing a 45-foot red tug and I'm looking right at you. What do you mean you can't see me? You blind or something?"

A different voice came over the radio.

"*I* can see you, Cap."

"That's nice, who are you?"

"Ocean Isle Bridge. You're right in front of me."

And so we were. That was years ago. In the meantime, we've changed our boat's colors and hailing port. But to this day, whenever she has to slink through either one of these bridges, Eddie makes me do the talking.

Off to the Races?

Although boats and bridges don't always mix well, at least one sailor managed to use a bridge to his own advantage. He was racing over a course which ran, at one point, through a swing bridge, something which the highway department would probably frown upon. He was in the lead and approaching the bridge when he discovered that it either wouldn't or couldn't open. Undaunted, he strapped in his sails, heeled down his boat, and sailed under with no room to spare.

Fortunately, I had already quit racing by the time I heard this story. It's been over ten years since I retired from racing, an anniversary that will doubtlessly be celebrated with more enthusiasm by those who crewed for me than by those who raced against me.

I started racing shortly after learning to distinguish port from starboard and found it an interesting experience. I discovered many important points about sailing and one important point about myself: at the sound of the starting gun, I am transmogrified from a pleasant, mild-mannered sailing companion into something resembling a female Ted Turner. Fortunately, by the time I met Ecks, my racing days were (temporarily, as it turned out) over. Thus, he never had the misfortune to encounter that particular dark underside to my personality.

My racing persona lay dormant until we moved south to the Florida Keys on *Serenity*, leaving *Whisper* behind on charter. I naturally gravitated towards the local sailing crowd, only to find myself being condescended to as a stinkpotter in a blow-boat world. I've never quite understood why, in an era when such bastions of middle-class mores as *Time* magazine casually discuss "bi-sexual chic," power and sail boat owners can't resolve their differences. But every time I tried to join a conversation, someone would say, "I was standing on the bow — that's what we sailors call the pointy end, Judy." I was not amused.

When these same sailors decided to start racing, we were invited to join mainly, I suspect, because of *Serenity*'s obvious potential as a committee boat. I accepted with alacrity and then went to retrieve *Whisper* before the committee boat topic could be broached.

Now, great emphasis had been placed on the notion that this was to be casual "Mom and Pop" racing, but that term had remained undefined until *Whisper*'s unexpected arrival. Suddenly, "casual" was synonymous with "no spinnakers." I argued that this was like saying "Let's all race but be careful not to go too fast," but everyone else seemed to be in favor of the ban. It wasn't until some time later that I determined that *Whisper* was, in fact, the only boat that *had* a spinnaker.

A more formal handicapping system, which appeared to be based in equal portions on boom length and voodoo, was also established. At first, I thought that *Whisper*, a CCA boat in an IOR world, had a good handicap, but then again, I always confuse large and small scale charts, too. Ecks finally explained to me, with the aid of charts, diagrams, and graphs, that *Whisper*, the smallest and oldest boat in the fleet, also had the dubious distinction of being the scratch boat.

The first race was held in August, a nice time of year in that part of the country if you like watching your shins sweat.

The mom-and-poppers, who were already beginning to sound more like Cup contenders than casual competitors, had decreed that the start would be based on Greenwich Mean Time, and they were all festooned with stopwatches and mumbling about "time ticks" a week before the race. I was more accustomed to thinking in cruiser's time — what day of the week is this? — and didn't own a wristwatch, let alone a stop watch. An intensive search of all our boats finally produced an old wind-up alarm clock, which we set to ALT, or approximate local time. We were ready.

Ecks started up his beloved Sea Gull outboard that served, however reluctantly, as *Whisper*'s auxiliary. It burst into ear-splitting life on only the tenth or eleventh pull, and we were off to the races.

Or halfway to the races, anyway. The Sea Gull, which had never run more than fifteen consecutive minutes, kept its record intact. As we made sail, I could see the other boats, their crews all resembling sea-going versions of Mr. T with their multiple stopwatch necklaces, timing practice runs. Eyeing my alarm clock wedged into a corner of the cockpit, I calculated that if we sailed full bore from where we were, *Whisper* would hit the line on time and on the favored starboard tack.

Now Ecks, as I mentioned before, had never seen me race and knew me only as an amiable cruiser prone to change sail. There-fore, as we bore down on the line, he felt it only reasonable to point out that I was on a collision course with a forty-five-foot ketch. Peering under the Genoa, I noted that the ketch was on a port tack, and, since *Whisper* had the right of way, I stood on. Ecks started making strange, strangled noises accompanied by fall-off motions. It was all highly distracting.

"I'm not on a collision course with him. He's on a collision course with *me*."

The increased decibel count from my crew made it obvious that he regarded this as the sort of hair-splitting that leads to hull-splitting. By this time, he had both hands over his eyes and had

115

apparently lost interest in the finer points of racing strategy as the sound of the ketch's bow wake drew ominously nearer.

"Bear off! Bear off!"

"That's how accidents happen."

The gun sounded, the ketch sheered off, and Ecks continued to whimper something about being shanghaied by a madwoman.

"Bring in the Genoa a little," I suggested, partly to distract him and partly to remind him that he wasn't out there for a joy ride, although I don't think that he had many illusions left about that.

"Good grief, not *that* much."

You could hear teeth grinding along with the winch.

"Can't you pay attention to what you're doing? Now it's luffing again. Where'd you learn to sail, anyway — from a correspondence course?"

"Sail your own damn boat. I'm going below."

"Stay out of the forward berth. I don't need another two hundred pounds of dead weight up there."

The only response I got was the thunk of hatch boards being slammed into place, followed by the thwack of a hatch. Some people just can't accept friendly criticism.

Believe me: I don't normally act like this. I don't like the sound of raised voices, particularly my own. I don't like sarcasm. I don't like arguments. But more than anything, I don't like to lose.

I was beginning to worry a bit about Ecks as we rounded the first mark, but soon I could see that the cowl vents were starting to turn, seeking some wind, and then the forward hatch cracked cautiously open. I promptly opened my mouth as well, ready to start yelling again, but determined, somewhat regretfully, that the hatch really wasn't open enough to affect *Whisper*'s aerodynamic efficiency. Obviously, Ecks was merely pouting, not prostrate.

After we had rounded the final mark and headed downwind on the home stretch, he was driven out of the cabin by the heat. Taking over the helm in the dying breeze, Ecks announced that we would stand offshore where we would find some wind.

"Inshore," I countered.

"Offshore."

Since I didn't have any idea where a breeze might be found, I was arguing only for the sake of being contrary. I finally yielded to Ecks's decision, and, followed by all the rest of the fleet save one, we headed offshore.

Ten minutes later, we sat becalmed atop our own mirror image, watching the inshore boat sail blithely along the beach. I was managing, with conspicuous effort, to maintain a rigid silence while watching a couple of jellyfish overtake us and sail by. I tried not to think about the spinnaker languishing in the forepeak. Sighing melodramatically, I leaned back and threw my arm over the cockpit coaming and onto a sun-scorched winch. Having "WOLRAB" branded on my forearm didn't improve my personality any.

A shimmering white spot on the horizon gradually resolved itself into the committee boat, although it seemed to be in the wrong place. I tried to re-check the race instructions, but since they promptly dissolved in my sweaty hands, I shrugged and headed for the supposed line. When *Whisper* finally crawled within hailing distance, a voice cried gaily, "We just came out to check on you." With that, they upped anchor and zoomed off to assume their proper position, with us following loggily in their wake. *Whisper* crossed the line in second place, and my cruising personality immediately reappeared.

"Let's drop the main and hoist the awning," I suggested cheerfully, making my first civil, and perhaps sensible, remark since the starting gun had sounded. I thought that I heard Ecks mumbling something about Mrs. Jekyll and Captain Hyde, but I couldn't be sure.

Since we couldn't afford both slip fees and a divorce lawyer right then, I thought that perhaps we should invite our friend Phillip to join us on the next race.

"But Phillip doesn't know anything about sailing."

"Well, that's one point in his favor right there."

The last thing we needed was another opinion on how the race should be run. Phillip had other, more valuable qualifications: his 250 pounds would make excellent movable ballast, and he could also serve as general scapegoat and buffer between me and Ecks.

On our way to the starting line the second time out, the dread Sea Gull ran its usual quarter hour and then blew its so-called muffler clean off. I hadn't thought that the Sea Gull could get any louder than it had been: I was wrong. The racket was more than any of us could bear, so out came the spinnaker. In a faint and diminishing breeze, accompanied by equally faint and diminishing hopes of reaching the starting line in time, we rambled on.

We came gliding down on the line from the wrong direction with minutes to spare and were greeted with a chorus of "No spinnakers!" from the assembled racers, who seemed to believe that we were planning to start the windward leg with the chute still flying. Dropping behind the line, we exchanged the spinnaker for the Genoa and re-crossed the line with the rest of the mob, several of them still mumbling protests.

My initial racing experience, I should point out, had been with a crowd that enjoyed only a nodding acquaintance with the racing rules, inasmuch as we had all fallen asleep while trying to read them. We had agreed that winning wasn't the only thing: survival was also considered a desirable goal, and to that end we did concede that the starboard tack boat would always have the right of way. Beyond that, anything went. Terrorist tactics were considered sporting, and as long as no collisions resulted, no protests were filed.

Therefore, I wasn't prepared for the mom-and-pop crowd, who raced with the tiller in one hand and the rule book in the other, and as *Whisper* worked her way past boats on the windward leg, I was accosted by remarks about "luffing rights," "mast abeam," and such. My standard response alternated between "But, of course" and "Try it." Our path through the fleet was soon marked by the protest flags in our wake.

But I was having a fine time, and Phillip's presence was having its desired effect. We were all still speaking to one another, even if no one else was speaking to us, when we surged across the line first.

Our reception at the post-race party was less than cordial.

"Maybe," one disgruntled pre-protest, pre-handicapping loser snapped, "you should consider reading the rule book, Judy."

"Maybe," I responded pleasantly, "if we're going to take ourselves so seriously, you should consider allowing spinnakers."

I had discovered that any mention of spinnakers had the same effect as a cross waved in front of a vampire. It worked again as this fellow backed away from me and towards the bar, hissing, "No! No spinnakers!"

For her third and final race, *Whisper* travelled to the starting line with the aid of a skiff and a 9.9 outboard, since I had determined that a twenty-six-foot sloop wasn't big enough for both me and a Sea Gull. (I didn't think it wise to offer Ecks his choice of which of us should stay and which should go.) Our friend Jack was supposed to be waiting to pick up our skiff near the starting line, but when we arrived, I could see his boat bobbing about a mile or so away. I called him on the VHF to find out what was causing his delay.

"Some damsels in distress," he reported cheerfully. I waited suspiciously for the rest of the story since Jack's humanitarian instincts had always been notably lacking.

"The wind's blowing so hard out here that it seems to have blown their bikini tops clean off."

Just what I needed: a couple of streakers on a Hobie. Jack agreed, albeit reluctantly, to come claim the skiff. Ecks was adamant, however, about not casting off the little boat until Jack was there to pick it up, so *Whisper* headed for the line with the skiff lunging along happily behind us like a puppy, a big, heavy puppy straining at its leash.

That soon proved to be the least of our problems. The same forty-five-foot ketch that had challenged *Whisper* at the start of

the first race was ahead of us, on a starboard tack this time. I
could see that she was going to hit the line early, but that wasn't
my problem. I was so busy timing my own start I failed to notice
the smoke that suddenly appeared under the ketch's stern or hear
the burble of her exhaust. I didn't even notice that she was
slowing down; and by the time that I realized that, even though
her sails were full and drawing, she was motoring blithely backwards, away from the line and towards me, it was too late.

She hit *Whisper* a resounding blow just aft of amidships, and as
my little sloop rounded up alongside the ketch, she wrapped our
skiff's painter in her wheel. This stopped the engine, and as we
drifted backwards through the fleet, I announced, among other
things, *Whisper*'s retirement from racing.

I thought that I was retiring from racing, too, but that was not
yet to be. The fleet had been swelled in the last couple of races by
a group of cruising boats, many belonging to friends who urged
me to join them with my other sailboat, *Syren*. I agreed.

Since *Syren*, a tiny schooner, had no engine (which I regarded
as an improvement over *Whisper*'s Sea Gull-plagued plight), we
got underway the day before the race and, leaving little to chance,
anchored for the night near the starting line.

The next morning, two distinct groups gathered at the starting
line. First came the big *C*'s — Cals, Catalinas, C&Cs, and such,
whose original mom-and-pop crews had given way, under the
same Bligh syndrome that I exhibited, to Pop and his pals, a
grim-faced lot bedecked with their ever-present stopwatches and
carrying their rule books.

Then came the little *c*'s, an engagingly motley assortment of
cruising boats that included Chuck and Eloise's big Warner-
designed motorsailor, *Fale*, a ferrocement Atkins-derived cutter,
Amigo, a Presto sharpie, a Meadowlark, a converted whaleboat,
and some others whose origins were shrouded in the mists of
time. Several of us, in an effort to appear more professional, thus
appeasing the serious racers, had strung alarm clocks around our
necks with flag halyard, but none of the hard-core types found

this gesture amusing.

Unfortunately, that was symptomatic of what had happened. Originally, these races were supposed to be casual and fun; instead they had become so serious and grim that the folks participating in the SORC looked like kids sailing toy boats in the park by comparison. The day that the group excitedly welcomed a new member, who arrived with his personal committee boat flag and a leather-bound copy of the rule book, I knew that the end was nigh.

It was nigher than I thought. We cruisers held back and let the "real racers" hit the line first, since there had been some surly remarks about "noncontenders" who "got in the way" at the start whenever a cruiser got the jump on one of his steely-eyed former friends. A couple of minutes after the formal start, our happy hodge-podge rambled over the line and set off to windward, or as close to windward as we could get, which was not always the same thing.

Syren and *Fale* began exchanging tacks and friendly insults. At our first crossing, we all waved amiably and traded complimentary remarks. At the second, we discovered that *Fale* had a bushel of oysters on board when her crew began pelting us with empty shells after we refused to yield the right of way. (In all fairness, I should point out that they did fire a warning shot across our bow first.) On our close encounter of the third kind, *Syren* returned fire with the only ammunition she had on board: banana peels and bologna. The bologna, which left a permanent polka-dot pattern on *Fale*'s scrubbed teak deck, was particularly successful.

Although we all eventually fetched the weather mark, we soon realized that, as far as our old gaffers were concerned, the next mark lay hard to weather, also. Cruisers are a flexible lot and, tired of tacking, we all agreed to do a 180 and run back for the line while "The Racers" thrashed on to windward.

The gaff-rigged, baggy-wrinkled, bowspritted *Amigo* promptly astonished us all by popping open a spinnaker.

"No spinnakers! No spinnakers!" we all chanted gleefully.

Our mock outrage was immediately echoed by the voice from the committee boat on the VHF, announcing the same thing in dead earnest and informing *Amigo* that she was disqualified.

Defiance spread through the fleet.

"More spinnakers! More spinnakers!"

A cheer went up as the whaleboat hoisted a tiny chute that was meant for something more the size of a Blue Jay. None of the rest of us had a spinnaker on board, but we all hoisted everything we could. Someone offered a bottle of Mt. Gay rum as a "most sails" award which *Syren*, flying jib, staysail, fore, main, topsail, and golly-wobbler, won handily.

Although none of our boats were exactly barn-burners to windward, they more than made up for this on the downhill slide, and soon we were bearing down on the committee boat in an avalanche of taut canvas. The race chairman, the same gent who owned his very own committee boat flag, grabbed his bull horn and attempted to re-establish his control of the situation.

"None of you have rounded the second mark and therefore you may not cross the finish line."

Well, the last any of us had heard it was still a free ocean. *Fale* and *Syren* pressed on, neck to neck or rather, bow pulpit to bowsprit, and it didn't take me long to figure out why Chuck kept squeezing my little schooner closer to the committee boat. As we drew abeam, he used *Syren*'s two masts to center his target.

"Fire when ready," we yelled, then ducked as a fusillade of oyster shells whistled overhead and found their mark.

It was the first and last shot ever fired in the Great Cruiser Rebellion. It was also the last time any of us raced in that part of the country. The mom-and-pop gang organized into an official yacht club, complete with rules, officers, committees — and blackballing procedures. Its first official act was to notify all the members of the short-lived rebellion that their participation in future races was neither necessary nor desired nor, for that matter, allowed.

And so it's been many years since I turned into a sea-going

shrew at the sound of the starting gun and, as I said at the beginning, I'm a happier person for it. So are my former fellow racers.

All Aboard

You may be wondering how a little boat like *Syren* was able to keep trading tacks with a big motorsailor like *Fale*. I'm tempted to let you believe that it was simply a matter of superior seamanship and skill on my part, but the truth is that *Fale* suffered from a handicap that my boat didn't. Chuck and Eloise lived aboard *Fale* and if they pushed her too hard, they had to deal with distractions like the potted plants falling over, or the kids being tossed out of bed during their naps.

You encounter a lot of new problems when you move aboard your boat, and many people are now writing books about living aboard to warn you about them. Although I have a great deal of faith in the written word, these books leave me with a few doubts. If I had read any of them fourteen years ago, I'd probably still be living on land.

Of course, this situation is not unique to boating. There are a lot of situations that none of us would ever have gotten into if we'd known in advance precisely what all was involved. These books, however, tend to focus on a lot of troubling questions that I chose blithely to ignore before taking the plunge.

For example, most of the authors go into painstaking detail regarding the rational selection of your live-aboard home. Personally, I find it difficult even to pretend to be rational about any aspect of boating, and I'm also a firm believer in allowing emotion to decide certain questions. I might as well: even though I'm forever making lists of the features that my next boat must have, I invariably fall in love with one that's lacking all these desirable characteristics. It's not unlike selecting a spouse. It would be nice if he or she were a rich, devastatingly good-looking orphan. But, alas, you're just as likely to fall for the poor, slightly buck-toothed only child of parents who believe that no one is good enough for their baby, especially not you.

Nevertheless, these guides go on at great length about the ideal live-aboard boat. Some even include elaborate formulas to determine "livability" that take into account the number of square feet divided by the volume of the icebox, minus the hanging locker space, or some such factor. Most of these calculations make the twelve-meter formula look like a second-grader's arithmetic lesson in comparison.

As I mentioned, I don't think that you can select the best boat for someone else any more than you could select the best spouse for a stranger, but I won't let that stop me from offering my one and only word of advice on the topic. Unless you're pathologically gregarious, never buy a boat that has more berths than you have permanent crew members.

As a live-aboard, you're likely to travel to interesting places with pleasant climes, where acquaintances who haven't passed the time of day with you in years are all too likely to show up, suitcases in hand, on the nautical equivalent of your doorstep as soon as they learn that you're spending February in the Keys.

If you have been foolish enough to buy a boat with extra berths, and especially if you have then compounded your error by bragging about how she "sleeps eight easily," you're in trouble. If, on the other hand, you have no spare berths, you can offer various insincere apologies about not being able to put these "friends" up

over night — or over winter — and direct them instead to the nearest motel. Then, as soon as they're out of sight, you can yank in your dock lines and split.

One other helpful note: if you do foresee the need for an occasional extra berth, try to fall in love with a boat that has her extra accommodations cleverly disguised. This way, your average landlubber will never realize that the dinette forms a double, if you just keep your mouth shut.

But finding your boat is just the first of many worries, according to these cheery books. What will you do with your lifelong accumulation of personal items? Sell them? Store them? Give them to relatives for a while, or for good? This was another problem that I didn't have to worry about. Some time before moving aboard, I found a different, but highly effective, technique for getting rid of excess baggage. I got a divorce.

This quickly reduced my household and personal effects to the extent that most of what I still owned would fit into a slightly-oversized handbag. Any time it appeared that I was going to get stuck with something I didn't really want, I merely informed Ecks that this was one thing that I simply couldn't live without. He rose to the bait every time and took immediate steps to assure his retaining possession of the "treasure." After all these years, I still wonder what he ever did with seven ice buckets, the "in" gift the year we wed, apparently, particularly the one shaped like a knight's helmet.

Then there's the question of what to do about having your mail forwarded. The books offer several suggestions: a formal mail forwarding service, an informal mail forwarding service (otherwise known as imposing on family and friends), having mail held at marinas or General Delivery, and so on. I briefly considered this mail "problem."

Then I thought about what sort of mail I'd been getting for the previous six months. As it happened, my personal finances, always rather shaky at best (those stories about writers starving to death in garrets did not invent themselves), were at an all-time nadir. My mail, as a result, leaned heavily towards envelopes with little plasticine windows.

Inside were ultimatums from the power company, the phone company, the stable where I kept my horse, my dentist, and various other creditors who were having second, third, and, in some extreme cases, final thoughts about my credit rating.

I had learned the sequence of collection notices from different sources, beginning with the perky pink ones that read, "We know that you're very busy and this is just a simple oversight, but your bill is a teeny bit overdue. When you have a spare moment, would you please send us your check?" and ending with the red ones that threatened to rip my phone off the wall, sell my horse for dog food, and pry the porcelain caps back off my teeth if I didn't show up with the cash in hand by noon.

Oh, there was other mail, to be sure. My congressman still kept in touch, and the local Piggly-Wiggly was another faithful correspondent. And there was always Ecks, the major mistake of my generally mistake-prone youth. (Not only mistake-prone, either, but prolonged, as well. Many people believed that I was going to be the first person to pass directly from adolescence to middle age without ever reaching the age of reason.) He wrote relentlessly, penning lengthy letters that protested his long-lost cause. He even offered to give me the knight's helmet ice bucket if only it would help. I amused myself by correcting his letters for grammar and spelling errors, grading them, and mailing them back with notes like "Poor organization, shaky research, too many generalities. Not up to your usual standards. C–."

However, since there hadn't been any mail worth reading in a long time, I had no qualms about simply moving aboard and sailing off without leaving any forwarding address. Maybe I was wrong: maybe the postman did show up with a check from the Publisher's Clearinghouse Sweepstakes the very next day. Somehow, I doubt it. So much for the mail problem.

What about the telephone? Sure enough, as the books point out, you can have one installed on your boat without much trouble, and many marinas stress the fact that they have phone hook-ups at every slip. But I've never understood why anyone would subject himself to the tyranny of the telphone when he has such a good excuse not to. It must be prenatal conditioning that makes us stop whatever we're doing, whether it's taking a shower, having an argument, cooking supper, or assuring the continuation of the human race, and leap to answer the phone's strident summons.

My general antipathy towards the phone wasn't helped by the fact that I was plagued with wrong numbers late at night. I don't know about you, but as far as I'm concerned, if the phone rings after 10 P.M., someone's died. But again and again, I'd be blasted out of a sound sleep long after midnight and answer the phone, only to hear an unfamiliar voice demand with drunken trucu- lence, "I want to talk to Bessie."

"I'm sorry but you have the wrong number."

The phone crashes in my ear. Back to sleep. Phone rings again.

"You put Bessie on that phone."

There's such a thing as raising your children to be too polite, and my parents had done it.

"I'm very sorry, but you do have the wrong number."

Why should I apologize? What had I done?

Crash again. Back to sleep again. Phone rings again.

"Listen here, woman, I know that Bessie is right there and I want to talk to her right now."

Eventually, I'd give up and take the phone off the hook, but this routine continued every weekend for over a month before inspiration struck.

"I want to talk to Bessie."

"Gee, what a shame, you just missed her. She and Jason left, not five minutes ago."

"Jason?"

"Sure, you know Jason, don't you? Tall, good-looking, drives a white Mercedes? Bessie said you were friends."

I won't bother repeating exactly what my mystery caller had to say, but he didn't bother me again, and I imagine that Bessie is still trying to explain that she doesn't even *know* anyone named Jason. At least, for her sake, I hope that she doesn't.

Of course, people other than Bessie's boyfriend called, but most often they were the same anxious folks who kept sending me the envelopes with the windows in front. The phone company itself called, threatening to do more than reach out and touch me if I didn't pay up. And Ecks, who believed that love means you never have to say goodbye, was another frequent caller.

Long before I ever thought about moving on board, I had stopped answering the phone. It was hard to resist all those years of training at first, but once I got over the initial hurdle, it got easier every time. When the phone shrilled, I would ask myself if there was anyone I felt like talking to. If the answer was no, I let it ring. I even found a little dial on the bottom that turned the volume down to almost nothing, and when this wasn't enough, I stashed the instrument under the bed. The only trouble I had with the phone after that was finding it on those rare occasions when I needed to make a call myself.

Incidentally, if you feel that you can live without receiving phone calls but not without making them, be sure to get a telephone credit card before you cast off. The phone company relies heavily on the threat of taking away your phone if you don't pay your bills, and once you've neutralized this threat, they can get rather antsy about extending credit.

The difficulty of having your money keep up with you as you travel also looms large in these live-aboard tomes. This was the furthest thing from my mind when I first moved aboard, since after buying the boat, I had absolutely no money left. Even now, my main problem is getting hold of the cash to begin with, and I have a hard time holding back a nasty, knowing snicker whenever I hear some potential live-aboard talk optimistically of writing about his experiences as a way of covering his cruising expenses. You would have trouble doing this if you limited your cruising to the Staten Island Ferry. If you don't believe me, you obviously haven't looked into the boating magazines' pay scales lately. Although being a free-lance writer is regarded as a romantic occupation, you should keep in mind that dying of consumption was considered romantic not too long ago.

Speaking of finances and romantics reminds me of an acquaintance who decided that he was going to cast off his shore-bound worries, quit his job, and find inner peace on a sailboat. The only flaw he could see in his plan was the $30,000 gap between his house equity and his dream boat's price tag, so he skipped right down to his friendly neighborhood banker and outlined his plan. To this day, he doesn't understand why he was refused the loan. Most bankers are practical business men, while most live-aboards have a romantic streak, and although the twain may occasionally meet, it's not likely that a loan will be made at the time. If you're looking to borrow money for your live-aboard home, I wouldn't recommend that you start off by showing the loan officer your charts of Tahiti.

You'd better make certain that your other sources of credit are squared away, too, before you announce your intention to take up the live-aboard life. I'd been a boat dweller for several years when I decided that a bank credit card would be a handy thing to have. Since I didn't owe anyone any money, I figured that I wouldn't have any trouble getting a card.

Have you ever tried to explain to a loan officer that, one, you have never borrowed money in your life; two, that you live on a boat; and three, that you're a free-lance writer? You might want to try it sometime, if you have a thick skin and enjoy watching someone indulge in a hearty laugh. This guy made it obvious that not being up to your high-water mark in mortgages and installment loans was positively un-American, living aboard a boat was one step below vagrancy, and that "free-lance writer" was just a fancy term for "unemployed."

I thought that this was insulting enough, but a few years later, I had an even more discouraging experience with Merrill Lynch. I was trying to open a money market fund when my broker asked me where I lived.

"On my boat."

"Uh oh."

"What do you mean, 'uh oh.' "

"They aren't going to like that."

I never did find out who "they" were, and the upshot was, in this case, that my living aboard had to be carefully glossed over, despite the fact that I was handing Merrill Lynch my money, not asking for theirs.

However, this experience was a help when I decided to try again for a credit card. This time I played the game "their" way. Under the question "Own home?" I checked off "yes." Under "Length," I almost slipped up and wrote "forty-four feet" but wised up in time to put "ten years" instead. I listed my address as "1 Dock Street," which was accurate enough since my boat was the first on the dock. As for "Employment," I upped my job description at the marina to "manager," which had a more reassuringly white-collar sound than the more accurate but more plebian "dockmaster." I also mentioned that I worked for one of the national boating magazines without delving into the freelance aspects of the relationship. And while I didn't claim to be editor-in-chief, I may have implied that this was more my decision than the publisher's.

Honesty may be the best policy, but prevarication proved to be the more effective one in this case. I got my card at last.

The writers of some live-aboard manuals erect yet another hurdle in front of would-be boat dwellers concerning the alleged difficulties of cooking afloat. I had read a number of nautical cookbooks prior to moving aboard, since people who went sailing with me once often offered such a book as a gift prior to accepting a second invitation. Most of these made depressing reading. The recipes could almost all be reduced to the same basic formula: one can of cream of anything soup, one can of meat or fish, plus salt and pepper to taste (these would have to provide the only taste), all dished up on a bed of instant mashed potatoes or instant rice. The "chef's" final comment was invariably, "Feeds four hungry sailors."

All I can say is that they'd *have* to be hungry to ingest these concoctions, which were always christened with jaunty nautical names like "Starboard Tack Stew" or "Halyard Hash," although a hash made *with* the halyards would probably be more savory.

After fourteen years of cooking aboard boats whose galley arrangements ranged from a single-burner folding Sterno camp stove and a portable ice chest to six burners, a double oven, and a walk-in freezer, I have reached just one conclusion about cooking afloat. It's like cooking on land, only you usually have fewer burners and a longer trip to the nearest grocery. This should not reduce anyone to a diet of canned goods, especially since the word "good" so rarely describes what you find in a can.

Having made this lofty pronouncement, I suppose that I should confess that my very first live-aboard meal consisted of hot dogs and canned baked beans, cooked in separate pots on a two-burner stove. I suppose the folks at *Gourmet* will now revoke my subscription. However, that was many years ago, and I've learned a lot about cooking on board, and cooking in general, since then.

Sea-going cooks do have some advantages over their land-bound counterparts. If you hate to cook, you can always throw your hands up in despair and announce, "How can you expect me to produce anything fit to eat in this ridiculous galley?" If you like to cook, you can expect to receive compliments far out of proportion to your efforts from people who are amazed at what can be produced from a well-planned galley.

I had lived aboard ten years before my parents ever set foot on one of my boats. Finally, they came to visit one Thanksgiving. I had cooked our usual full-scale dinner, with roast turkey, two dressings, gravy, rice, candied sweet potatoes, asparagus with hollandaise sauce, homemade yeast rolls, and two pies for dessert. All during the meal, my mother kept reminding my father, "She cooked this whole meal *all by herself!*" I don't know what she thought I'd been eating during the fifteen years since I'd left home — Starboard Tack Stew, I guess.

I don't think that my father was overly impressed with my lifestyle, however. After dinner, we were sitting around in the wheelhouse, watching my parents' new Scotty pup, Robby, terrorize my cats and chew up deck shoes. My mother and I were talking while my father watched the news.

"We probably shouldn't have bought another dog at our age. What if he outlives us? What'll happen to him?"

"Don't worry, Mom. If anything happens to you, I'll take good care of Robby."

My father looked up in horror.

"Robby can't live on a *boat!*"

Despite my father's doubts, about the only trouble I've encountered with cooking aboard arises every Thanksgiving and Christmas, when I have to remember to take a ruler to the grocery store with me so I can be sure that the turkey will fit in my boat's miniscule oven. I once made the mistake of buying a bird that was a bit too big. The skin was too close to the hot oven wall; first it blistered, then it charred, and finally it exploded, spraying the oven with molten turkey fat and creating a memorable mess.

As long as we're in the galley, what about plates? While weekend sailors may make do with paper, I can't imagine anyone wanting to eat off them on a regular basis. For a change, I started life afloat on an unexpectedly elegant basis in this one respect with a set of Royal Copenhagen china. When, after a few years with *Serenity*, I acquired the blue-water cruising cutter, *Eleuthera*, I stashed the china and invested in unbreakable seagoing plastic dishes that had a rubber ring around the bottom and were guaranteed not to slide off the table at angles of up to forty degrees.

That was a nice thought, but I failed to take two factors into account. For one thing, although the plates did stay put as advertised, what was on them did not. If a regular plate, loaded with spaghetti, comes loose from its moorings and takes a flight across the table, you do have a slight chance of catching it. If, on the other hand, the plate stays put while the spaghetti itself is launched into space, about all you can do is try to get out of its way.

That was the first problem, and other than serving only very sticky foods that would glue themselves onto the plate (and then onto your palate), I never found a solution. But I had also failed to consider another factor that made these plates useless. Any time conditions were such that plates took flight, which sounds rather like one of the descriptions on the old Beaufort scale, I didn't really feel much like cooking, let alone eating. I went back to the china.

Not too long ago, I met the author of one of these live-aboard manuals who told me, although I hadn't asked, how to go about rigging an antenna for my television set. I didn't have the heart to tell him that, at that time, I didn't have a set on board and hadn't had one for several years.

Somehow, I have never been a television junky, although if you threatened to stick cotter pins under my fingernails, I might admit to having rushed home from school during one particularly mis-spent period of my youth to watch "American Bandstand." But I didn't really care much about television, and since I first lived aboard in Key West, where even network TV reception required a cable hookup, I did without. I couldn't see paying money to have yet another line binding me to shore.

Over the ensuing years, I discovered that if you don't have a television, you tend to fall utterly out of step with the rest of the population. I must have been the only person between the ages of two and dead in the 1970s who didn't know why everyone was going around saying, "Here comes de judge," and for a long time I was under the impression that "T&A," which I heard was on all the channels, must be a new rock group.

I probably wouldn't have a set today if my parents hadn't grown tired of my saying things like, "What do you mean, Nixon's not the president any more? The elections aren't until next year." They bought me a dandy little set that runs on 110-volt

AC, 12-volt DC, a set of self-contained batteries, and, for all I know, butane. My favorite program is the weather. I turn off the sound, look at the map and satellite photos, and try to guess what the weather girl's sweeping hand gestures are supposed to mean.

Finally, only a few of the live-aboard guides address the subject of pets. I was fortunate in at least one respect: I didn't own a dog when I decided to move aboard and have avoided acquiring one in the meantime. Despite the familiar expression "salty dog," it doesn't seem that man's best friend was cut out for the cruising life. Over the years, I've watched unhappy canines lunging into dinghies, lumbering up companionways, and leaping desperately onto the dock after a day spent far from trees and fire hydrants. Also, for some perverse reason, the size of the dog always seems to vary in an inverse ratio to the size of the boat, with three Newfoundlands residing on a twenty-six-foot sailboat while a teacup poodle, whose rhinestone collar weighs more than he does, dwells in solitary splendor aboard a seventy-two-foot Burger.

I did, however, own, or at least share my living quarters with, a pair of alley cats. I had considered moving aboard the twenty-six-foot *Whisper* before I took just one of these cats on board to try it on for size. You may be familiar with the carnival act billed as "The Walls of Death," where motorcycles race madly round the inner walls of a cylindrical building. Well, that's precisely what the cat started doing. I began searching for a bigger, a much bigger, boat.

If you've been reading carefully, you may recall that I made mention some pages back of a horse. Here was a problem that I have yet to see mentioned in the most thorough live-aboard manual. What does one do with a 1,000-pound Arabian mare? Who happens to be pregnant with, as it turned out, twins? Do you install extra heavy-duty davits and carry her across the stern in a sling? Buy a small barge, fence it in, and tow it behind you? It took me two years to accept the inevitable conclusion that she would have to be sold. And although I still have two cats — one is presently sitting atop the VHF, shedding great clouds of hair which will soon get inside the radio and lead to another $72 repair bill, while the other is draped around my neck, hoping that I'll soon leave the typewriter and head for the can opener — if I had to recommend the ideal live-aboard pet, I'd have to vote for a more lethargic choice. Something along the lines of a hermit crab, or perhaps a pet rock.

And still, after spending a third of my life living on board a boat, I can't help wondering where I'd be now if I had read about all the alleged problems and pitfalls that lay ahead when I made my boat my home. I still think that living aboard is like a lot of other decisions that many of us simply slide into rather than actually make. Whether we're thinking about getting married, having children, or changing careers, maybe we're better off not knowing exactly what all the consequences of our decision will be, just coping with them as they come along.

And They
Lived Happily
Ever After

Most couples who contemplate living aboard have been strongly influenced by the ads in the yachting magazines that show tanned, smiling couples lolling about on their gleaming, polished yachts, which are anchored in calm, crystalline blue waters. You can almost hear the palm fronds sighing in the background as one of these couples stare soulfully into one another's eyes. Romance isn't dead, it lives on in the boating ads and in the hearts of would-be live-aboard couples.

It's easy to forget that life afloat has its drawbacks. When you first think about living aboard, you picture tropical islands, forgetting about tropical hurricanes. You long for the simple life, forgetting that it sometimes involves lugging jugs of kerosene through a cold rain down an endless dock. You long for solitude, forgetting that you can wind up anchored at Catalina with half the population of Southern California. You dream of getting back to nature, forgetting that nature sometimes has a way of getting back at you. You picture yourself and your spouse on an eternal floating honeymoon and forget to bring aboard the most important thing a live-aboard can have, a sense of humor.

I remember one starry-eyed couple who cornered me in the boatyard while I was scrubbing a year's accumulation of flora and fauna off the bottom of my old Matthews. There I was, the quintessential live-aboard; duckwalking under *Nity*'s broad, flat after sections, thigh muscles reduced to quivering jelly, arms and clothes covered with soft, red copper bottom paint, and hair matted with unidentified marine growth.

"You've sure got the life," the woman sighed enviously. "Just think, no more floors to scrub."

Even this woman, however, was at least one step ahead of many women who wouldn't even consider moving onto a boat. Their reluctance to adopt this lifestyle is understandable. For most men, living aboard their own boat is a lifelong dream that began when they were little boys playing with their toy boats in the bath tub. With a real boat of their own, they can at last think of themselves as The Captain instead of the third assistant to the second junior vice-president in charge of public affairs.

The distaff perspective may be a bit different. A woman may also be reminded less favorably of her own childhood when she contemplates the tiny sink, minuscule stove, miniature icebox, and seventeen square inches of counter space that supposedly add up to a galley. Making mud pies with toy kitchen equipment as a little girl is one thing: being expected to produce real meals with it as an adult is another.

Some wives absolutely refuse to consider life afloat and make the fatal announcement, "You're going to have to choose between me and that damned boat," in the apparent belief that their husbands are going to grab the phone book and start looking up yacht brokers. More than one such wife has discovered, alas, that she's not even a close second and that the number her husband is looking up is an attorney's, not a broker's. Any woman who's thinking about throwing down this particular gauntlet should be aware that there are plenty of happily married men living aboard and cruising contentedly — with their second wives.

A smart wife will accompany her husband when he goes boat hunting, if only to protect her own interests, but this still doesn't guarantee a successful transition. When I put *Serenity* up for sale, a couple, both supposedly enthusiastic about taking up the boating life, came to look her over.

I gave the woman the basic tour and then waited for a barrage of questions about the galley (small), the hanging lockers (smaller), and the shower (non-existent). But nary a question was raised until just before they left when she turned to me and plaintively asked, "But where do you do your ironing?"

Ironing! You mean they still make irons? You certainly couldn't prove it by me. I suspect that the few ladies out there who are still ironing aren't the same ones who can adapt to the casual, crumpled live-aboard life.

A few years back, a friend brought his understandably dubious fiancée aboard my boat to show her that living on a yacht could be perfectly normal. *Eleuthera* had been built with living aboard in mind, so she was both pretty and practical, with lots of varnished mahogany brightened with white paint, teak cabin soles, Delft tiles in the galley, polished brass oil lamps, and other pleasantly homey touches. Seeking to make a favorable impression, I brewed some freshly-ground coffee and served warm, homemade apple pie.

Everything was going quite well until Susan went to rinse her coffee cup in the sink. Her cup crashed to the floor and her blood-curdling scream echoed throughout the anchorage as two salamanders popped out of the drain and slithered up onto the counter. Shocked by the commotion they'd caused, the two terrified salamanders zipped back down the drain, but I was never able to convince Susan that I'd never seen them before — or after, for that matter. She seemed to believe that slimy creatures in the sink were an inevitable part of living aboard. The next time I saw Susan and Peter, they were studying house plans.

Although some of your friends will envy you, your families may be less than supportive when you opt for the boating life.

Younger live-aboards have parents who want to know when they're going to grow up and get a mortgage like everybody else. Older couples have to listen to their grown children make snide remarks about second childhoods and acting their age. Middle-aged folks, as usual, get it from both sides.

Therefore, when my friend Chuck's sister came to visit from America's own heart of darkness, Chicago, he and Eloise wanted to make sure that everything went well. After all, his sister would be reporting back to her parents on what type of living conditions their only two granddaughters were enduring. The boat was cleaned to a fare-thee-well, the menus carefully planned, and the kids forced to put on shoes. Everything was going according to plan until Chuck, while showing his sister how to work the head, managed to pump a very lively and very indignant squid into the bowl. Sis immediately elected to use the shore facilities for the remainder of her stay and returned to squid-free Chicago considerably ahead of her original schedule.

It's always easier to laugh at other people's problems, but when you move aboard you're bound to encounter a few of your own that don't seem so amusing. Just getting used to cramped quarters takes time, and although it may be easy to brush off the first collision you have with your spouse when you arrive at the companionway simultaneously, the third or fourth time an elbow lands in your ribs, it's easy to decide that it's a deliberate provocation.

One of the first things you'd better learn to do on board is control your temper. When the cook neglects to put the sea rails on the stove and an unexpected wake hits and flips the steaks onto the cabin sole, it's better to brush them off, keep on cooking, and make a joke about "filet of sole" than to rant, rave, and cast blame on one another before tossing dinner overboard.

There simply isn't room, physically or psychologically, for much arguing on a boat. If you're underway, you have more important things to do. If you're in a marina, you're likely to have an amused audience eavesdropping, and if you're at anchor, you have no way to escape from one another while tempers cool.

The effects of close confinement coupled with bad weather shouldn't be underestimated. I remember a summer in Key West when we were having an exceptional run of vile weather, with an hour of violent thunderstorms followed by an hour of steaming, scorching sunshine, then another storm, and so on. This storm-and-steam seige lasted for days, and there was nothing to do but sit and watch the mildew create new patterns as it spread across the overhead.

Chuck and Eloise were spending these grim days trying to get ready for a long-awaited cruise to the Abacos. One afternoon I almost collided with Eloise in the grocery store as she whipped her cart around the corner on two wheels. Failing to notice the malevolent energy with which she was flinging canned goods into her cart, I foolishly asked how things were going.

"One more word out of Chuck and I'm going to tell him to take the boat and the kids to the Bahamas by himself and *stay* there," she snapped.

I was shocked. Sure, I knew couples who talked like this all the time, but not these two. I backed off cautiously, making appropriately soothing and sympathetic noises, but actually feeling smugly superior. After all, *I* wasn't letting a little bad weather ruin *my* disposition.

When I got back to my boat, Ecks and a couple of other guys were sitting around the cabin telling tales of high adventure on the high seas, or perhaps, since their conversation stopped abruptly when I came aboard, they were comparing low adventures on the low seas. Their gam was soon interrupted again by the arrival of another live-aboard wife, who announced in decidedly shrill tones that the head was backed up and overflowing again, and if her husband didn't get back to the boat and fix it *right* this time, she was going to open all the seacocks and let the damned thing sink before catching the next plane home to her mother.

Really, I thought. The way some people make public spectacles of themselves is just a shame.

The battleground then moved to a small sloop that was anchored off our stern. I don't know what spark set this couple off, but soon the anchorage echoed with shouts of, "You're getting more like your mother every day," followed by, "Well, Mother was sure right when she told me not to marry *you*." The skipper stomped out into the cockpit, jumped into the dinghy, and rowed furiously around the boat several times before going back aboard. Round two was soon underway and wasn't finished until another squall drove the contenders back below.

I was still laughing about this latest display of pique when Ecks joined me. Before I could tell him about this latest battle in the live-aboard wars, he snarled, "Where's the ogee bit for the router?"

"Well, let's see, the last time *I* used it . . ." I began, but he rudely interrupted me with some churlish remark about the boat being such a mess that he could hardly find the bulkheads, let alone a router bit that *he* had certainly put back in its regular place.

Sure enough, within ten seconds we were shrieking at each other like everyone else. It wasn't very funny at the time, but now I can see the joke. Of course, having divorced the grouch in the meantime probably helps.

In fact, if truth-in-advertising ever makes its way into the yachting magazines, we'll still see the pictures of the loving couple smiling into one another's eyes aboard their thirty-six-foot cutter. But behind them, we'll see a fellow smiling into his checkbook aboard a ninety-foot Burger. Who's he? He's the divorce attorney who has his offices right next to the marina.

Labor Day

If living aboard can prove hazardous to your marital health, living aboard while your boat is hauled out is almost a guaranteed ticket to divorce court. My husband, Eddie, and I have continually tempted Fate by taking the Boatyard Blues one step further: we always haul at least one of our boats over Labor Day Weekend and spend the "holiday" laboring. In the hands of two less battle-scarred veterans of the domestic wars, this would be sheer insanity, but we manage to get away with it.

Last year, we decided that since we had both been working unusually hard for months, we had earned the right to turn over most of the dirty work to the boatyard crew. We both agreed on this and then arranged to haul out over Labor Day weekend so that we could, as always, get everything done ourselves. You would think that one of us would have noticed a slight contradiction here.

We talked over our plan to haul *Irish Rose* with the owner of the local boatyard, who had previously hauled only one houseboat, and that a particularly flimsy model. It had proved unable to support even its own weight and had promptly settled down on its keel like a broody hen. The yard owner, Zero (so called because he's one of the few men in town who isn't at least a III or IV) had eventually managed to wedge enough blocks under that specimen to paint her bottom, but he had also vowed that he would never haul another houseboat.

It took us a while to convince him that *Irish Rose* wasn't really a houseboat, but rather a steel barge that just happened to have a house built on it. We weren't too surprised when Zero agreed to give it a try. Although ninety-five percent of the boats that he hauls are large shrimpers, his was also the only yard between Spencer's and Derecktor's that was willing to haul a 1930s vintage twelve-meter. He hauled this venerable beast once, and then issued a "no 12-meters" ban to go along with the "no house-boats" edict. Of course, this ban didn't have much effect on Zero's business, twelve-meters being decidedly few and far between in McClellanville, South Carolina.

We had planned to haul out on Friday afternoon, but a local shrimpboat sprang a leak and needed some emergency attention. With the thermometer heading for the upper nineties, we hadn't been having too much difficulty controlling our enthusiasm for this project to begin with and were more than gracious about yielding our turn.

Saturday found us still ready, or at least resigned, to haul out, but the railway carriage stuck and would lower only halfway before it jammed. We recalculated the tides, figured that it would be late Sunday at best before we could get out of the water, and decided to put the whole project off until the next week, or next month, or the next Labor Day, for that matter. Instead, we decided that we would take the catboat out for a sailing picnic.

That plan was abandoned when Zero woke us before daybreak on Sunday with the news that he had been up all night fixing the railway and was now ready to haul us. It didn't seem an opportune moment to tell him that we had changed our plans.

Before I had managed to get both eyes open, we were out of the water; I don't know how it is for other people, but I always seem to have some sort of unpleasant surprise awaiting me when one of my boats is hauled out. You know, the worm shoe has disappeared, or the centerboard needs blasting, or some other such unwanted diversion. *Irish Rose* proved no exception. I knew that her bottom paint had died sometime earlier, but what I hadn't realized was that it had disappeared entirely. Surprise!

If you read the paint company ads, you know that they love to talk about "systems" of painting. This is especially true when you're dealing with steel hulls, which require at least three separate stages of preparation: a wash, an undercoat, and a topcoat of anti-fouling. We had, at considerable effort and expense, used one such complete system on *Irish Rose* during her last haulout, but the system had failed. From her waterline down, there wasn't a trace of paint left.

What we found instead was a shellfish crop that was a fine tribute to the fertile qualities of South Carolina's silty, salty, nutrient-rich waters. Barnacles as big as fifty-cent pieces crowded oysters the size of my hand for the available space on the houseboat's broad, flat bottom. It was painfully apparent that we would have to chisel these creatures off, one by one, and then sandblast the boat again. The cost of this haulout, whether measured in terms of dollars, hours, or blisters, was rising like a Titan missile.

Zero, who was more accustomed to deep-draft commercial boats, eyed Irish Rose's pancake bottom with disbelief.

"Flounder'd be a fool to try to follow her," he chortled. It wasn't hard to see that he was happy to be well out of the situation when he handed us a couple of implements that resembled straight-headed hoes, pointed to the sharpening wheel, and fled to a holiday family cookout.

I stared at the weapon he had placed in my hand and called to his retreating back, "What about building a fire under her and having an oyster roast instead?"

He pretended not to hear me, so I turned and glowered at Eddie who was, after all, the one who liked steel boats to begin with.

"And just what, exactly, am I supposed to do with this?"

I suppose that I should give him credit for refraining from giving me the obvious answer. Instead, he flipped the "hoe" upside down and took a swipe at *Rose*'s shell-encrusted bottom. A small shower of barnacles fell, but not nearly as fast or as far as my spirits. It was beginning to look like a long holiday.

I took up my hoe and began hacking. Although the barnacles let go without too much of a struggle, every time the hoe encountered an oyster, my arms were jolted half out of their sockets. It would then take five or six sideways swings to pry each bivalve loose. I soon became aware that I was scraping skin off my hands faster than I was scraping shells off the boat.

I shinnied up the ladder and onto the deck, hurrying to get my hands bandaged and get back to work. I bounced through the wheelhouse quickly and didn't realize, until I tripped down the companionway into the galley and zipped right past the head door and into the stateroom before finally fetching up with a thud in the after companionway, that the boat was perched at a considerable angle.

In addition to the slope of the railway itself, *Irish Rose* also draws more at the bow than the stern, leaving a total effect not unlike a ski jump. I struggled back uphill to the head and thoughtlessly flung open the medicine cabinet which was mounted on the forward bulkhead. A hailstorm of cough syrup, shampoo, shaving cream, and other sundries launched itself at my head, bounced off the after bulkhead, and landed at my feet. Digging the bandages out of the rubble, I patched up my hands and fled the scene.

Hoe in hand, I returned to work. By this time, I had reached the point where my boat reached her maximum fourteen-foot beam and her minimum eighteen-inch draft, and my quivering forearm muscles confirmed that I was working against gravity, if not the very nature of the universe itself. There was no easy way to tackle the job. If I started scraping near the chine and worked my way inboard, I had to crawl over a layer of sharp, broken shells. If I started near the keel and worked my way out, it was easy to slice my back or scalp open on the same razor-edged shells while they were still attached to the hull. And no matter which way I went, I had to grovel about first in sand and mud, and then, with the incoming tide, in salt water. Shoal draft is wonderful when you're cruising, but God help you when your mud-skimmer is hauled out.

By the time I reached the final third of the hull, I had also reached a personal nadir of misery and was beyond caring about pain and exhaustion. I believe that long-distance runners call this hitting the wall; I felt more like the wall had hit me. I was sick of attacking barnacles and engaging oysters in one-on-one battle with the aid of a chipping hammer. My back was bleeding from dozens of shell cuts, my hands were covered (after the fact) with salt water soaked bandages, my muscles were screaming from the contortions required to crawl over the railway carriage while simultaneously ducking under the hull, and my temper was as raw as everything else.

If you're in the market for a forty-four-foot houseboat, you missed your chance; I would have sold her on the spot for any reasonable offer. And by four o'clock, my definition of "reasonable" had dropped to anything in the four figure range and two of those figures could have come after the decimal point.

With the battle of the bivalves over, we turned our attention to some half-hearted grinding of the hull wherever rust had blossomed through the paint, then daubed red lead over these wounds before they could start bleeding rust again. Back when we had bought *Irish Rose*, I had jokingly suggested that we name her with the Swedish word for "restless": *Onrust*. It didn't seem as funny any more.

Before long, we lucked up and the rising tide forced us to quit for the day. I was discouraged, to be sure, but things weren't bad enough that I wanted to stand in salt water up to my knees while running an electric grinder.

Our original plans had called for our retreating to the marina at this point for long, soothing showers, then dining out at a nearby restaurant. Our original plan, however, hadn't called for our participating quite so fully in the grungier aspects of the haulout.

Gathering up towels, soap, shampoo, clean clothes, iodine, and more bandages, then trudging off to the marina seemed like more work than it was worth, so we elected to shower on board.

The shower drain was, naturally, located forward, and the shower pan was shallow. We soon adapted to the necessary routine to prevent flooding: shower a minute, kick water uphill to drain for a minute, and then repeat. With the accumulation of rust and mud we had to remove, this took some time. I also learned that it's remarkably difficult to shampoo oysters out of your hair.

Although the showers brought about considerable improvement, the tangy aura of a South Carolina mud flat at low tide still hung about us. The additional effort required to make ourselves anything near socially acceptable seemed more arduous than cooking aboard, so I broiled up a couple of burgers in my lopsided galley.

Our Labor Day labors got off to a refreshingly late start, thanks to our being the only boat in the yard. On every other haulout, unkind fate had placed me next to an early bird who greeted the dawn by mincing up oak four-by-fours with a dull circular saw. I broke a couple of eggs into the skillet to fry, only to have them slide down to the low side of the pan where they turned into eggs *à la* wedge. We ate them anyway and flung ourselves back into the fray.

We had decided that we would tackle the job from the chines up, since the rest of the bottom work would have to be turned over to the yard's sandblasting crew. We ground the rest of the hull down to bare metal, washed it with an acid etching solution, hit it with two coats of red lead, and finished it off with a glistening top coat of glossy dark green. We finally found one advantage to working in ninety-five degree heat, in that the paint dried almost immediately and we could cram three day's worth of painting into one, if our arms held out.

The problem was that all our good, big, natural bristle brushes were on our tugboat, which was fifty miles away. This left us with nothing but tiny, wretched nylon-bristle throw-away brushes to work with. Theoretically, these brushes were to be used only once. In practice, this wasn't necessary, since they shed so many bristles that they virtually self-destructed within the first hour's use. Also, the largest brush we could find was a two-incher; trying to paint a forty-four footer with one of these was like trying to clean the typical boatyard head with a toothbrush.

Another charm of these brushes was their inability to hold much paint. Loading up the bristles enough that you could paint more than four square inches at a time meant that a fair amount of paint flew off at the end of each stroke. This wasn't much more than another annoyance until Eddie and I both reached the bow of the boat from our opposite sides and got within range of one another. When you're already feeling a bit testy from sweat running into your eyes, acid etching into the previous day's collection of cuts and blisters, and muscles aching from a day of scraping followed by another spent lugging around a twenty-pound bucket of red lead, it's surprisingly easy to misplace your sense of humor when your mate lobs a glob of Malachy green paint into your ear.

My final job of the day was cutting in the name and hailing port on the stern. I've painted enough boat names over the years to know that the same job that looks dreadful at a distance of six inches looks fine when you back up six feet, but I still get frustrated every time. What is more, the audience that invariably gathers doesn't help my composure any.

This time, I was working in hip deep water, and every minute or two some form of hungry marine life would either slither against my leg or nip me on the toe. My painting efforts were therefore punctuated with unpredictable yips, yelps, and leaps, which my audience found most amusing.

Fortunately, I finished painting the name at about the same time that daylight and my patience both wore out. As usual when you're halfway through a haulout, the boat looked worse than ever. *Irish Rose* was a blotchy mess of old and new paints and primers.

Discouraged, I stumbled up the ladder, marched through the grit-filled pilothouse, and announced, "I'm all for a drink, a sit, and a shower, in that order." Eddie pointed out, as diplomatically as possible, that perhaps the shower had better come first, since at some time during the day, I had already had a "sit" in red lead. And I was wearing shorts. Toting along my jug of paint thinner, I dragged my weary bones into the shower.

I was so tired that I took my shower while sitting on the cabin sole, discovering only later that I had left an indelible smear of green paint at shoulder level on the white bulkhead as a permanent reminder of the occasion. I threw on a terry cloth robe in lieu of drying, then poured myself a glass of rum, threw in a chunk of lime, and declared it a Daiquiri before starting dinner.

"Oh, boy," Eddie grumbled from his comfortable perch in the pilothouse, "hamburgers again."

I shot him a look that was a sufficient reminder that the alternate menu for the evening was likely to be hot tongue and cold shoulder. You'd think that he would know better than to antagonize a woman with a frying pan in one hand and a chipping hammer in the other.

We crawled into bed early. The previous night we had had trouble sleeping, since the head of the berth was aft, and we felt like we were trying to sleep while standing on our heads. This night, I had re-made the bed with the pillows at its former foot. We fell into a deep, exhausted, dreamless sleep for a while. And then the ship's cats, who were used to sleeping at the foot of the bed, came bouncing in.

Having a fifteen-pound ball of fur jump on your head is startling enough, but when it then lets out a strangled, surprised cat shriek, things really get exciting. Eddie yelled back, and the cats fled to the pilothouse. About the time we got back to sleep, they had decided that it was all some sort of mistake and hopped up again. This performance was repeated throughout the night.

I was glad when morning arrived and Eddie still hadn't followed through on his threat to launch the cats without the boat. When the yard crew reported to work, I had a pretty good idea of how the cavalry felt when reinforcements came riding over the hill, although the cavalry probably wasn't churlish enough to wish that the help had waited until after sunrise to make their appearance. Leaving me in charge, Eddie left for his office with unseemly haste, trailing hollow promises to be home early.

I had mixed emotions about the yard's taking over. One of the highlights of my last haulout with *Irish Rose* had taken place when the yard in question had reversed their earlier decision to allow us to use our own welder and insisted that we employ their man instead. This might not have been so bad, but after he had worked on our boat for less than an hour, his welding machine died, and we spent the month of July on the hill waiting for it to be repaired. That was infuriating enough, but the final straw came when the yard handed me a bill for over $700 in lay-day fees.

I was not the least bit amused. In fact, I later wrote an article which mentioned some of this problem, and since I didn't want to use the yard's real name, (actually, I would have loved to, but the editor, with visions of libel suits dancing through his head, wouldn't), I opted instead for the sobriquet "Filth and Greed Boatworks." The editor wasn't crazy about that, either, but it made me feel better.

Happily for us all, Zero's yard was different. While dear old Filth & Greed would still have been cutting the work order, Zero's men had the bottom blasted and the first coat of primer on. By midafternoon, they were finished, and by the time Eddie got home, the entire job was done. Compared to her last haulout, this was like watching one of those time-lapse movies which show a flower sprouting, budding, and blooming within a matter of seconds. We spent one final night on the rails while the bottom paint cured, then went back overboard in the morning.

The old bucket looked good. She was still nothing to make your heart beat faster, and there wasn't any danger of my walking right off the end of the dock while I was admiring her over my shoulder, as I'd done with one of my previous boats. But as my friend Chuck used to say, "A little putty and a little paint will make the old gal what she ain't."

We loaded up all our supplies of paint, primers, acids, scrapers, tools, cleaners and rags, and, trying not to think which of our other boats was also due for hauling, headed for home. Another Labor Day weekend was over.

Born to Save

I overheard a conversation between two boating wives the other day that got me to thinking. One boat was having engine troubles, and the lady from the other boat was quick to offer help.

"If Dan needs any special tools or anything, tell him to ask Tim. He's probably got everything you'll need in his little blue box."

The other woman sighed wearily and said, "I'm afraid that what we need is a new port engine."

"That's all right. I'm sure that Tim's got one of them stashed somewhere."

After thinking this over for a while, I realized that every experienced boatowner that I know has his own equivalent of that little blue box. Experience makes pack rats of us all. It's the old "for want of a nail" syndrome done over in nautical terms. For want of a cotter pin, the mast was lost, and so on. Boat owners, particularly the ninety-nine percent of us who are on a tight budget, quickly learn never to throw anything away.

After a couple of years, you find yourself in my position. I open a hanging locker and three sets of leaky foul weather gear fall out. I pull out a galley drawer, or, to be more precise, *the* galley drawer, and have to shuffle through a half-dozen snap shackles to find a knife. I try to locate a chart on my catboat and have to dig through stacks of out-of-date Tide Tables and ancient "Notices to Mariners." And the lazarette — well, the lazarette just doesn't bear thinking about. I can't imagine anything less valuable than the Hope Diamond or smaller than a Volkswagen that I'd even try to find in there.

Sometimes more reasonable folks suggest gently that I dispose of this accumulation of trash and treasures, but I've learned only too well the first law of boating: The day after you throw something out is the day you finally discover a need for it, which means that you'll have to buy a replacement for it at — God help us all — full retail.

Over the past few years, Eddie and I have owned an assortment of boats that ranged from an eight-foot sailing dinghy to a 136-foot minesweeper, and our resulting collection of gear covers the same gamut. Take anchors, for example. For Christmas, I received a folding grapnel for my dinghy that weighed in at 1.7 pounds. (It can also be used as a watch fob in the off season.) At the other extreme is the tug's 500-pound Danforth, obviously an anchor of the last resort. I suppose that if things ever got so bad that we needed this behemoth, we'd have enough adrenalin flowing to get it over the side somehow, but I can't imagine how we'd ever get it back aboard. Between these two extremes are about a dozen more anchors, and every spring I swear that I'm going to sell off a few of them. Fortunately, I suffer from an extreme case of inertia and never get around to doing this before hurricane season, when approaching storms find me thinking more in terms of buying extra anchors than selling the ones I already own.

This anchor hangup may be a personal idiosyncracy, but I also save other items. If there's a common denominator among pack-ratting boatowners, it's probably paint. Think about it for a minute. Do you or do you not have at least a dozen almost empty cans of paint stashed around your boat, dock box, car trunk, and/

or basement right now? I thought so. Surely I'm not the only one surrounded by everything from tiny pots of gold leaf for gilding name boards to five-gallon buckets of red lead and white undercoat?

I used to think that this paint problem was the sole province of wooden boat owners, but right now I own nine boats, only one of which is wood. Of course, my situation is complicated in that four of these boats are green, three are white, and two are black, not to mention their different deck and trim colors, three different types of bottom paint for glass, steel, wood, and aluminum, two types of varnish, and all the necessary thinners and brush cleaners.

I always swear that the next time I open a can of paint, I'm going to keep right on painting until it's all used up, even if this means that part of the boat gets two coats while the rest gets three. In practice, this never quite works out, and I wind up with still more leftover paint.

There are a number of methods for dealing with this problem. You can throw a lit match in the can and quickly slam the lid on in the hopes that this will burn up the oxygen that causes the paint to skim over. I know that if I tried this, the fumes would explode, or, failing that, sooner or later I'd discover that burnt match, doubtlessly in a finish coat.

Other possibilities include taking a deep breath and exhaling into the can (oxygen depletion again) or cutting a circle of waxed paper to cover the surface of the paint, or, for you belt-and-suspenders-*and*-elastic waistband types, doing all three. I'm not well enough coordinated to try this triple play myself. I know that I'd end up with my lower lip shut in the lid while the match set the wax paper ablaze, leaving me to die of smoke inhalation.

I've never had much luck with any of these methods. The only sure way I know of to save paint is to purchase clean, new cans from the paint store and decant the leftover paint into them so there's little or no air space left. This works, but unfortunately, I'm too cheap to pay good money for empty cans. I waste good paint instead, a fine example of false economy in action.

In addition to dribs and drabs of dried-up paint, I also maintain a strong inventory of used sandpaper. You can use a sheet of sandpaper for only so long before you realize that it's not working at peak efficiency any more. Out comes a new sheet, but what do you do with the old one? I mean, it's just too good to throw away, isn't it? It's still good enough for some small job, right? When you reach this stage, do yourself a favor and do as I say, not as I do: Throw it away. Believe me, this sort of thing snowballs on you. One day you've got two slightly used pieces of wet-and-dry, and the next thing you know, you're being driven out of your boat by boxes of worthless sandpaper, dull saw blades, and petrified paint brushes that can be used again only as chisels.

This brings us to tools. The typical sailor's toolbox is the repository of screwdrivers with chipped blades (which would be useful for prying open those cans of hardened paint if only you could find one when you needed it instead of reaching for a good screwdriver — the blade of which you promptly chip), a few pairs of pliers that have rusted solid but which you plan to free up some day, dull chisels that you plan to sharpen on that same never-to-be-seen day, and at least one pair of locking pliers that doesn't. In the bottom of the box we can count on finding several used hacksaw blades, broken drill bits, a large collection of unmatched nuts and bolts, and several fouled spark plugs. These are just the basics; most of us like to add our own personal touches.

Then we have sails. These must be the hermaphrodites of the boating world. You throw a couple sails in the forepeak and two weeks later, you find six of them up there. Maybe that explains all those strange rustling noises coming from up forward in the middle of the night.

It seems to be my karma always to acquire boats that have one suit of working Dacron sails and a large inventory of old cotton sails that her former owners couldn't quite bear to discard, either. I recently met the latest owner of one of my old boats and asked him what had become of her Egyptian cotton sails, which I'd always regarded as too fragile to use but too beautifully made to throw out.

He admitted that, like me, he'd suffered many an uncomfortable night crowded out of the best accommodations on the boat so that these useless but elegant sails could be properly pampered. Unlike me, however, he had finally reached his breaking point during a long, wet slog to Bermuda.

"I hoisted the first one at daybreak, and it promptly blew out. The second one lasted almost an hour, and the third a little longer. By sunset, they were all gone, and I had a dry berth for the night."

I offered him my heartfelt congratulations.

"Of course," he added sheepishly, "I couldn't quite force myself to blow out the sheets as well."

I groaned, and he looked properly chagrined. The little boat's old sheets were made of manila that was every bit as soft, white, delicate, and useless as her cotton sails.

"Well, I may make fenders out of them some day," he added defensively.

There probably isn't a sailor alive who hasn't made that same excuse at least once while a locker, if not an entire garage, gradually fills up with stray bits and pieces of line. Everyone's hanging on to at least one stretch of nylon dock line that's so stiff that you don't have to throw it to the dockhand. You just stomp an eight- or ten-foot section out straight and hand it across without its so much as sagging.

I once bought an entire coil of line so stiff that it should have been cut into short sections and used for boathooks, dinghy spars, and reaching struts. The old Indian fakir's trick of climbing an unsupported rope never held any mystery for me after I'd dealt with six hundred feet of this stuff. As a reminder to be more careful when buying "bargains" in the future, I forced myself to use it all, but I did try whenever possible to drop it into oil-slicked water, tie it to heavily creosoted pilings, and arrange it for maximum chafe. It wasn't long before I could honestly say that I needed new lines, but you know, I still couldn't bring myself to toss the old ones into the nearest trash barrel.

Instead, I bludgeoned them into coils (no small task in itself), and added them to my collection, which ranges from a spool of flag halyard, which I'll use one day if I can ever remember to install a cheek block on the catboat's mast when it's down for varnishing, to an unknown quantity of four-inch towing hawser. In between are coils of old halyards, topping lifts, sheets, docklines, anchor rodes, and, alas, some ridiculously short pieces of line that are totally useless. I mean, what do you do with an eighteen-inch long piece of three-quarter-inch nylon other than tote it around in the bottom of the ditty bag for five years, which is what I've done so far?

New line also has a strange effect on sailors. Back when I built *Eleuthera* from a bare hull, I decided to splurge on new line for everything. I stacked up coil after coil of this soft, white, wondrous stuff and felt richer than Croesus, although I was poorer than a church mouse after paying for it. Any time I felt depressed, I'd look at my new line and dream of dock lines that could be coiled and thrown, anchor lines that didn't peel the skin off my hands, and sheets that could be wrapped around a winch without the aid of a pipebender.

But I simply couldn't force myself to make that first cut. For weeks after *Eleuthera* was launched, I kept her secured with scavenged bits of old pot warp and twine, putting off the inevitable day of slaughter.

But an approaching winter storm finally forced my hand, and I discovered something strange: once you've made the initial cut into a new coil of line, you go into the equivalent of a shark's feeding frenzy and can't stop yourself from whacking off great chunks of line on the slightest whim. It's quite possible to be able to recall cutting only two one-hundred-foot halyards off a coil but find the spool almost empty. It's something like breaking a hundred-dollar bill — the change is gone before you know it.

Out of all those reels of line, all I have left is one hundred feet of half-inch yacht braid. And for the past six years, I've been sailing my catboat *Faith* with a half-inch yacht braid main sheet that's about fifteen feet too short. This led to some interesting experiments in sailing by the lee before I developed my present practice of tying the free end of the centerboard pennant to the tag end of the mainsheet, a practice which doesn't exactly fall within the bounds of good and prudent seamanship.

The problem is, if I cut into the new line to make a new mainsheet for *Faith*, I'll be stuck forever with about fifteen feet of leftover line which I'll never find a use for and which I'll have to make room for in my coffin when that day arrives. And if I use the line without cutting it, I'll spend more time coiling down the sheet than sailing. And finally, there's no way I can justify buying another piece of line that's the right length when I've got more than enough line already sitting in a locker.

In contrast to *Faith*'s too-short mainsheet, there's my sailing dinghy's mainsheet, which is about three times as long as it need be. I've got a perfectly good explanation for this, too: the dinghy's mainsheet is also *Whisper*'s spinnaker sheet. I sold *Whisper* in 1973, but I still can't bring myself to cut up her lines.

I guess that it's hopeless. Sometimes I try to cheer myself up by thinking that someday I may buy a boat that needs precisely one hundred feet of half inch yacht braid, or maybe I'll buy another Pearson Ariel that's missing a spinnaker sheet. But I'd probably be better off if I just accepted the truth: Some of us may be born to lose, but if you're a boataholic like me, you were born to save.

The Cure

When I first realized that boataholism was ruining my bank account, if not my life, I went overboard and wound up with only my eighteen-foot catboat, *Faith*, and her nine-foot sailing dinghy, *Begorrah*. As a single-hander, *Faith* had her virtues, but I was also living aboard her if, as my father was wont to say, you could call that living. She lacked not only standing headroom but sitting headroom as well, leaving her with what might charitably be called crouching headroom. Her already tiny cabin was neatly bifurcated by the massive centerboard trunk which took up about ninety percent of her cabin sole. And her galley was a bit limited, although after a year of living with it, I'm sure that I qualified as the Julia Child of the Sterno set.

This was about the time I met Eddie, whose taste in boats ran more to large steel tugs than tiny glass catboats, and who thought that people were supposed to work aboard boats and live ashore. After years of living aboard, I thought just the opposite. At one point Eddie mentioned, in an attempt at compromise, that he knew of a houseboat for sale. At the very mention of the word, my upper lip curled into a sneer: Heaven forbid that I should ever own a *houseboat*. I stood my ground — or crouched on it anyway — aboard *Faith*.

And then one February night the soft splitter-splatter of falling rain on deck changed to the pitter-patter of driving sleet. I cranked up Faith's little electric heater and retreated to the sleeping bag. Sometime during the night, I was awakened by a fog of cold, damp air creeping into the cabin. Peering out an ice-covered port, I realized that the powerlines were down. I crawled deeper into my sleeping bag, only to be awakened again when *Faith* took a violent sideways lurch punctuated with a sharp "crack."

Convinced that the bow line had parted, I leapt up, struck my skull on the overhead, tripped on the sleeping bag, hit my head again on the centerboard trunk, and finally covered the total distance of three feet to the hatch. It was all a waste of effort; the ice had formed a thick, unbreakable glaze over the entire boat, and the sliding hatch was frozen shut.

By the time that Eddie arrived in the morning with an icepick to chisel me out, I had had more than adequate time to reconsider my previous stance on houseboats, and by evening, we were the owners of the forty-four-foot *Irish Rose*. And although buying her was the boataholic's equivalent of taking a shot of medicinal brandy, I must admit that I was somewhat intoxicated by the fact that she was basically a sound, well-built boat that was merely in desperate need of some work. While the alcoholic looks at a drink and thinks, "I just need this one," the boataholic looks at a boat and thinks, "This one just needs me." I'm not sure which illusion is more dangerous, although I have a pretty good idea which is the more expensive.

Surprisingly, the purchase of the houseboat failed to set me off on another boat-buying binge, and for a couple of years, we held the line at only five boats. This may seem a rather hollow boast, sort of like saying you got drunk every night but never quite passed out. But for a recovering boataholic like myself, it was quite an achievement.

I found my downfall in the classifieds. I had continued to read the boat ads, partly out of habit and partly because there isn't much else to read in a small-town Southern newspaper unless you're interested in hog and soybean futures. Anyway, most of the boats listed for sale were sixteen- or eighteen-foot outboards with giant, thirsty engines. I had no use for these, believing as I did that it was a shame to mess up a perfectly good boat with smelly dead fish, and that if the good Lord had meant us to ski over the water, He would have given us longer, flatter feet. So I continued blithely reading these ads with all the fervor of a reformed alcoholic perusing a wine list, and eventually the inevitable happend.

"Cape Dory 10, needs mast, $200." A phone number, which I was already dialing, followed.

Like most boataholics, when I find a boat that I want, I immediately fall under the delusion that everyone else in the tri-county area is also trying to buy it. Therefore, when no one answered the phone, it was obvious to me that the boat had already been sold and the owner driven out of his home by the incessant calls from other buyers. After all, the paper had been on the stands for over a half-hour. But I kept on dialing and planning my strategy.

I've bought a lot of boats over the years and have developed several hard and fast rules. First, never appear overanxious. Next, look the boat over carefully before making any offer. Finally, never pay the asking price.

About the 832d time I called, a man answered. I looked over my long list of questions that should be answered before I drove the 140-mile round trip to look at the boat and started in.

"I guess you've already sold the Dory at that price."

I couldn't believe I'd said that.

"No, I just got home from work and you're the first person that's called."

"Is she all in one piece?"

"Well, she's a little rough, but . . ."

165

"Never mind, I'll buy her. Someone will be there around six to pick her up."

I sure do drive a tough bargain. I barely remembered to get the directions to the owner's, make that former owner's, house, and then called Eddie. By this time it was all over, as they say, except for the shouting.

"You can't possibly have bought a boat without even seeing it!"

"How can you say that when I'm telling you that that's exactly what I just did?"

There was some more colorful conversation in this same fruitless vein before Eddie agreed to pick up my new prize on his way home. But he really is just as hooked on boats as I am, and by the time he got home, you'd think that the Dory had been his idea to begin with.

Boataholics tend to see things as they could be, not as they are, and so we saw the Dory with her blackened woodwork refinished to bring out its rich mahogany glow, and the lumpy blue paint on her hull replaced with smooth, gleaming dark green. All it would take would be a little paint and varnish and a month or two of my time. But first came sea trials. We dragged the little boat unceremoniously down to the creek's edge and shoved her in.

I rowed away from the lights of the village and then pulled in my oars and let the little boat drift through water so calm that the stars were reflected on its still, black surface. Far to the south, the loom of an approaching tugboat's spotlight flared and faded, and from the east came the low boom of the surf that rolls ceaselessly off Cape Romain.

I finally stopped making mental lists of the scraper blades, sandpaper, and varnish that would be needed to bring the dinghy, already christened *Rosebud*, back to life, and simply enjoyed the night. Like most of us, boataholic or not, I often wish that I had more free time and fewer worries, but for a while, I was at peace with myself and my boat-filled life. But soon I noticed that the tide had turned and was carrying us out one of the creeks that led through the salt marsh to the open Atlantic, so I turned around and headed for home with the oars cutting smoothly through the water. Being a boataholic, I decided, wasn't all bad.

And Then A Great Wind Came

It was a dark and stormy night that got me off the catboat and onto the houseboat. It was a darker and stormier night when I made my next move.

I had sailed around the southeastern United States for sixteen years without ever getting anywhere near a hurricane. That suited me fine, although I realized that the odds were likely to catch up with me one day. All I asked, if I had to be in a hurricane's path, was that it arrive during daylight and low tide.

And then came 1985. The hurricane season started early, and soon Tropical Storm Bob was heading my way. The Experts — why do I still listen to Experts? — assured us that Bob wasn't going to get his act together in time to become a hurricane. As a matter of fact, the Experts assured us that we wouldn't get winds over forty miles an hour. Eddie and I continued eating dinner. We keep our boats secured for winds that strong all the time.

At 6:28, the Experts reappeared on screen and informed us that *Hurricane* Bob would hit us around midnight. We threw our dinner dishes in the sink and dashed outside.

Our main problem was three boats tied up near us. Their

owners were out of town. We grabbed our own lines and fenders and secured these boats as best we could. One of them, a twenty-four-foot houseboat, was lying alongside *Irish Rose,* with my catboat, *Faith,* also tied up to the *Rose* ahead of it. We usually kept the catboat where the little houseboat was, but we didn't think the houseboat could survive a storm tied to the dock, so we kept it alongside us. Our big tug was at the far end of the dock, while the *R.R. Stone* was tied up behind us. We did what we could in the little time we had before dark.

The electricity went off around dusk, and before long Eddie announced, "I'm going to bed."

"You're kidding."

"No point in both of us sitting up worrying."

A few minutes later, he was snoring peacefully. An hour later, his snores were being drowned out by the rising wind.

As the wind moaned and shrieked and wailed, I had trouble fighting the tendency to moan and shriek and wail along with it. The houseboat pitched and lurched, and even the windows began to vibrate with the force of the storm. The worst noise came with the individual squalls, which announced their arrival, with ninety-mile-an-hour winds, with a sound like a freight train or a tornado approaching.

The storm reached its peak at two in the morning, which was, of course, the time of high tide. The dock disappeared under water, cutting off our escape route. We were still all right, but I couldn't help wondering if things were going to get worse. For four hours, the wind continued unabated.

At four o'clock, there was a horrendous crash, and the houseboat lurched so hard that lamps fell over. That woke Eddie up, all right. The two-foot diameter ball that we'd placed between *Irish Rose* and *Faith* had come loose, and the wind was forcing the catboat's bow under the houseboat's. As they rose and fell in the four-foot chop, the houseboat smashed repeatedly onto the little boat.

We yanked on foul weather gear and tried to get out on the

forward deck, but we couldn't open the door against the force of the wind. We finally got out the back door and crawled forward to wedge more fenders between the boats.

We had just stripped off our wet clothes when the crashing began again. Since Eddie can't swim, I made him stay inside the houseboat and hold the light for me as I again slithered up the side deck on my belly, pulling myself along with *Irish Rose*'s welded steel lifeline stanchions. Trying to keep my hands and feet away from my wildly lurching catboat, I crammed more fenders into the gap.

The fifth and final time I went out that night, I had used up all my dry clothes and didn't see any point in pulling on my soaking wet foul weather gear again. As I crawled out the door in my underwear, Eddie looked shocked.

"Hey, you can't go out there like that!"

I was in no mood to argue about niceties.

"It's 4:45 in the morning and there's a hurricane blowing. Just who do you think I'm going to run into? Charles and Di?"

I crawled back into the houseboat minutes later, spitting salt water and thoroughly defeated. I had used the last of our fenders: if the wind didn't ease up soon, the houseboat was going to tear the side out of little *Faith* and sink her. Eddie went back to bed, while I took up my vigil in the pilothouse again. I wasn't exactly sitting there singing "There's Got To Be A Morning After," but I wasn't too far from it, either.

Just after daybreak, the wind finally shifted and eased, and I crept into our soggy bed. After a few hours sleep, I got up to assess the damage.

The big boats were all right, but the little catboat that I'd sailed for seven years without a scratch had taken a beating. Most of her oak rub rail was gone, and some of her fiberglass toe rail had been destroyed. We could repair the damage, but it still hurt to look at her.

What bothered me more was the complete lack of judgment that I'd shown in risking arms and legs to save a boat. This was exactly what I'd been telling other people not to do for years, but when push came to shove, I'd done it myself. And I was afraid that I'd do it again.

Later that day, I noticed Eddie writing a check and putting it in an envelope.

"What's that?"

"I'm sending away for the house plans."

Several years earlier, we'd bought a piece of land at the headwaters of our creek and picked out a house plan. We had always planned to build there some day: *some day* had arrived.

We started out by building a combination workshop and garage, where we could store our accumulation of boat gear and tools while building the house. This started out as a simple, basic structure, but that didn't last long. Soon, a one-and-a-half-story New England salt box began to grow in the woods. Any time our energy levels would flag, another storm would whistle our way, and our tempo increased. The rafters, studs, walls, and floors of the building were soon covered with cryptic notes that marked the paths of the half-dozen hurricanes that developed while we were building. We would hammer and saw by day, design and draw by night.

Friends who stopped by to watch our progress kept making the same two remarks.

"It looks more like a house than a garage."

"This place is big enough to live in."

It wasn't until Hurricane Gloria headed our way with 150-mile-an-hour winds that the light dawned. We had quit working early enough to catch the evening news and turned on the television just in time to hear Dan Rather announce in solemn tones, "The storm of the century is bearing down on the Carolinas tonight." We listened glumly as Dr. Neil Frank of the National Hurricane Center burbled enthusiastically about how exciting this storm was. (I sometimes think that the only thing harder to endure than a hurricane is Dr. Frank's chipper reports of how exciting, interesting, or unusual a particular storm is.) Although he assured us that the storm would turn north and accelerate, I couldn't help thinking what would happen if it decided to accelerate first, since we were directly in its path.

By 6 A.M., it was still heading our way. Having seen what even a "minimal" hurricane could do, Eddie and I were forced to accept the fact that if this monster hit us, we could very well lose everything we owned.

Gloria missed us, but the die was cast. We began finishing out the interior of our little house in the woods so we could live in it while building the main house.

I was learning a new language as we built. Plates and joists, sills and cripples took the place of frames and carlines, deck beams and clamps. The ceiling was once again what went over your head, and the floor was once again what you stood on.

On my thirtieth New Year's Day, I had launched my cutter, *Eleuthera*, which I had built. On my fortieth New Year's Day, we moved back ashore into the little house which we'd built. The first of the stories that make up this book were written on a manual typewriter on *Eleuthera*'s saloon table. Others were written as I crouched aboard *Faith* with the typewriter on my lap. The last ones were written on an electric typewriter on *Irish Rose*'s dinette table. The final manuscript, however, is being written on an electric typewriter on a desk in our new, land-bound home.

But my boats will never be far away. On one wall is a picture of the gray sloop *Whisper*, with her red, white, and blue spinnaker defiantly flying. Next to her is what looks like an aerial view of *Serenity*, caught during a spectacular roll on her way back from Dry Tortugas. And then there's one of *Syren* doing what she always did best — looking beautiful. Another photo shows a stern view of *Eleuthera* silhouetted against the dawn, bound for the Charleston Sea Buoy — and distant waters. On another wall is my favorite picture of *Faith*, slipping downwind through one of South Carolina's salt water creeks on a sunny summer evening. *Irish Rose* is shown tied to the dock, with the barbeque grill smoking and a box of geraniums blooming on the forward deck. And finally, our two 1930s vintage tugs, *Judith R* and *R.R. Stone*, are shown steaming confidently through the water, each with a dredge in tow.

Out my back window, I can see the waters of Jeremy Creek, which has sheltered my boats for years. Out another window, I can see the bows of my two sailing dinghies, *Rosebud* and *Begorrah,* sitting on their racks. And out the front window, I can see little *Faith* sitting on her trailer, waiting for us to heal the wounds caused by Hurricane Bob.

But I don't need this to remind me of my boats. They've all been a part of my life. There isn't one of them that I haven't cussed at least once, and there isn't one of them I wouldn't take back in a minute.

But for now, I seem to have found a permanent mooring. Or maybe it's not so permanent, after all. Every time someone looks over our house plans and asks, "How much do you think it'll be worth when you're finished?" I smile and think of distant waters and answer, "I'd say it'll be worth, oh, about the same as a trawler. A real nice, forty-five-foot trawler."